Suzanne,

To a leader wh
already in sl
for teaching us ..

Voted most improved.
The real leader in you
is a shining light

Getting Into
Leadership
Shape

Published by Mindstir Media, LLC

1931 Woodbury Ave. #182 | Portsmouth, New Hampshire 03801 | USA

1.800.767.0531 | www.mindstirmedia.com

Printed in the United States of America

ISBN-13: 978-0-9975435-9-9

Library of Congress Control Number: 2016906652

Getting Into
Leadership
Shape

With 15 Exercises to Strengthen Your Character and Competence

Janet McCracken, CEO
Ed Beard, President
Employers Edge, Inc.

MINDSTIR MEDIA

What Leaders are saying about
GETTING INTO LEADERSHIP SHAPE

"The biggest impact our leadership can have on the success of our company is to develop and maintain a culture that aligns with our values. Getting Into Leadership Shape™ gives us the path for our leaders to engage in conversations around character competencies that are bigger, richer, and have more meaning. These conversations inspire connections, accountability, and bring people in alignment with the organizational purpose. The exercises in this book will be extremely useful for our managers and our emerging leaders."

Tony York, CPP, CHPA, *CEO of HSS Inc. and Coauthor of Hospital and Healthcare Security*

"Getting Into Leadership Shape™ is a must read for anyone on your leadership team. The exercises will help develop your leaders and leave them wanting more." What I find refreshing about this book, is Janet and Ed's ability to provide practical, hands-on, real world application in their teachings and exercises. Their stories reveal the same types of problems that some of my leader's experience. This book is the tool box and action plan that I need to effectively follow up with my leaders."

Suzanne Deremo, *Chief People Officer, LPR Construction*

"People always ask me if they are "naturally wired" to manage people. Thanks to *Getting Into Leadership Shape™*, I can give them this book which will help them on their path to managerial and leadership success. Like the book mentions, no one is worthy of managing others until they have mastered the art of managing themselves."

Randy Austad, *President of Follow Your Calling*

"As an engineer and CEO, I evaluated the usefulness of a tool by the level of its application to my world and its effect on the bottom line. *Getting Into Leadership Shape™* is a compilation of the exercises used by Janet and Ed in coaching and developing the current and future leaders in my company; exercises that people can immediately apply on the job, in their leadership roles to better build teams, and develop their people. Under Janet's and Ed's tutelage, we achieved record growth and stability during an economic recession. And we changed people's lives."

Lisa Negri, *past CEO of LT Environmental and philanthropist*

"This book will help you get and stay in leadership shape as an executive, manager, emerging leader or business coach. The powerful and practical exercises in this book has made a huge impact on myself and my company. Now our leaders are not only in "leadership shape", but we have created a more engaged workforce. It has made my business life far less stressful."

Richard R. Frank, *CEO of Lawry's Restaurants*

"Getting into Leadership Shape guides us through the traits and attributes of effective leadership. This is a book 25 years in the making. It takes the concepts of leadership and makes them into utilities that interested readers can apply. The stories will remind you of yourself or someone that you work with and the exercises will help you develop your leadership strength. Please enjoy the journey."

Kevin E. Thompson, CPA, *President of Thompson CPA*

"I have worked with Janet McCracken and Employers Edge for 15 years utilizing evaluation instruments, group trainings and individual customized training and development programs for people ranging from middle to executive management.

The results have been consistently astoundingly good. Leaders come away with a strengthened resolve to perform, and more importantly, to lead from the perspective of servant leadership. If you are looking for assistance to effect a culture shift to a performance based learning organization, look no further. This book is an actionable "how to" manual with exercises to strengthen your resolve and develop leadership awareness and habits that will ultimately develop your leadership performance."

David Patterson, *Partner at dwespconsulting, LLC and past President at US Foods, Inc.*

"The message is simple…exercise your leadership! Don't think that knowing how to improve your leadership is the same as actually doing what it takes to be an effective leader. To get and stay in leadership shape, you have to complete the exercises in this book regularly."

Robert Kirch, *President at Variety Pet Foods*

To Chris, Scott, Alyssa, Taylor, and Bucky
Our children and future leaders

To our clients from the past 25 years
who taught us how to create long-lasting leadership change

To our friends and editors,
Kathy Groom of Groom Development
and Gretchen Goldsmith of Rose Publishing
who helped us turn our stories and teachings
into a book worthy of reading

CONTENTS

Introduction: **EXERCISING YOUR LEADERSHIP**   11

Getting Started   16

Leadership Self-Assessment   20

Chapter One: **LEAD WITH COURAGEOUS CONFIDENCE**   29

Are you making the move or controlling the fall?

Exercise #1: Crash Pads   46

Exercise #2: Conditioning Impact   50

Chapter Two: **LEAD WITH TRUST AND RESPECT**   55

Can someone trust your competence and intentions?

Exercise #3: Talk Straight   72

Exercise #4: Trust Questionnaire   74

Chapter Three: **LEAD WITH INTEGRITY**   78

Do your words and actions match up?

Exercise #5: Values Exercise   95

Exercise #6: Boundaries Exercise   99

Chapter Four: **LEAD WITH COMMUNICATION AND MANAGE CONFLICT**   102

Are you a "ME monster" who talks more than you listen?

Exercise #7: The Interpretation Exercise   121

Chapter Five: **LEAD WITH ACCOUNTABILITY**   126

Do you take responsibility for your mistakes or do you blame others?

Exercise #8: The Blame Game Exercise   138

Chapter Six: **LEAD WITH INFLUENCE**   **142**

Are you leading or taking a walk?

    Exercise #9: Giving Positive   161
    Feedback Exercise

    Exercise #10: The Seven Appreciation   162
    Styles Exercise

Chapter Seven:**LEAD WITH A FUTURE FOCUS**   **168**

Do you focus on the vital few instead of the trivial many?

    Exercise #11: The Goal Planning   180
    Process Exercise

    Exercise #12: Where I Stand Now Exercise   185

Chapter Eight:**LEAD WITH SELF-DISCIPLINE**   **190**

Are you spending time in activities that are
worth more than your rate of pay?

    Exercise #13: High Payoff Activities Exercise   208

    Exercise #14: Stressors Exercise   210

    Exercise #15: Emotional Response Tracker   212

Chapter Nine: **LEAD YOUR ORGANIZATION BY CREATING**   **215**
               A LEADERS DEVELOPING LEADERS CULTURE

Are you creating an environment in the workplace
that develops leaders?

INTRODUCTION:
Exercising Your Leadership

*Think of yourself as an athlete and go
practice your way to leadership perfection!*

It starts with a reason; it always does. Some reasons are bigger than others and some reasons have a meaning only known to us. In the world of sports, for example, every athlete getting into shape has a reason to exercise—to gain speed, strengthen target muscles, surpass the competition. Leadership can be thought of the same way.

If you are serious about wanting to get into leadership shape, then you will need to exercise. This book will give your leadership a workout, retrain your leadership muscles, and improve your leadership cardio. Developing the eight leadership competencies in this book will get you into shape as a leader, and when you commit to the exercises at the end of each chapter, you will not only get into leadership shape, you will stay there.

In sports, no one would argue that some sports enthusiasts are naturally more athletic than others. In leadership, some of us are more naturally gifted leaders than others, but anyone who exercises leadership will end up a better leader than had he or she not exercised at all.

What is your reason for getting into leadership shape? To gain a promotion? Or have you been placed in management and need to develop the skills to excel? Do you want to learn how to be an accomplished leader because your non-profit organization's cause is important to society? Or is it simply that you have a life value of self-improvement and want the personal satisfaction of challenging yourself? Whatever your reason for wanting to be a better leader, when you exercise your leadership abilities you will improve.

Whether you consider yourself a born leader or not, let's accept who you are and go to work on it, and let's accept who you are not, and go to work on that. The key to success for any leader or manager, whether born for leadership or not, is the continued and relentless

11

development and awareness of personal leadership competencies.

We define competencies as the abilities, traits, behaviors, and knowledge needed to perform a job, or in this case, to be an effective leader or manager. Competencies fall into one of two groups—Skill Competencies or Character Competencies. A leader can be competent in a skill such as delegation, developing staff, or managing projects because he has learned that skill. But if a leader is not effective in character competencies such as trustworthiness or self-discipline, then chances are the skill competencies will bring about marginal performance.

Over the past twenty-five years, The Employers Edge, our organizational development and talent management company, has been tracking the character and skill competencies that are most frequently causing leaders to fail or fall short of expectations in their leadership role. Below is a table of the competency weaknesses we have seen, based upon coaching over 8,000 leaders in 400 client companies. The % reveals the competencies that have been in the most need of improvement. We have coached numerous leaders on how to exercise and grow in these areas in order to get better results for the organization. In most cases, leaders needs improvement in an average of three to four areas at any specific time during their career.

LEADERSHIP COMPETENCY COACHED	% COACHED
Communicating and Conflict Management	89%
Influencing and Motivating Others	65%
Coaching and Developing Teams and Staff	62%
Planning and Goal Setting (strategic, workforce, departmental, and personal)	44%
Personal Integrity and Accountability	38%
Building Trust and Respect	37%
Project, Time, and Task Management	33%
Self-Discipline – Self Control – Managing Emotions	32%
Confidence and Courage	22%
Collaboration/Partnering	22%
Hiring and Interviewing Effectively	21%

Delegation	16%
Understanding Performance Management Processes and Practices	15%
Sales and/or Presentation Skills	14%
Life Balance and/or Stress Management	9%
Managing Change/Adapting to Change	8%
Problem Solving and Decision Making	5%
Developing Vision, Mission, Values, and Culture	4%
Political Savvy	3%
Leveraging Diversity	3%
Business Acumen and Entrepreneurship	2%
Thinking Creatively	1%

Getting Into Leadership Shape focuses on the top eight character competencies identified as most important in the chart above. These competencies are essential to being a good leader, because ultimately, a leader has not earned the right to lead others unless he or she has learned to manage his or her own character. Unfortunately, many leaders are unaware of their own strengths and weaknesses, stuck in bad thoughts and habits.

Some leadership development experts would suggest that character traits such as integrity or trustworthiness can't be developed. That is to believe that once you fall short, you will always fall short. Don't ever accept that! We will show you in the pages to follow how you can develop your character and improve your leadership through the exercises that we will teach you. You can master leadership skills by developing and exercising whichever character competencies you see need improvement in your own life.

Inside the exercise is the experience.

It is the vehicle to reveal the strength, the weakness, the next step. When you exercise, your reason behind it shifts from a powerful wish to an identifiable purpose. A good exercise grows and stretches us into something even bigger and more meaningful than what we could have even imagined at the start.

It's important to recognize the importance of using proven and well-defined exercises. For example, fitness trainers will put together a specific regimen geared towards a goal and use proven methods to attain that goal. This same regimen is also needed with leadership development. We need to have an experienced and skilled leadership coach who will help us see where we stand on the leadership competency scale and give us a plan with exercises based upon our goals. We will help you do that! Through our assessment in this book, we will help you identify your leadership strengths and weaknesses, pointing you to the most appropriate exercises for you. By setting a well-defined plan with specific exercises designed to improve your character competencies, you will gain undeniable strength and effectiveness in your leadership skills.

Keep in mind that the need to develop a particular leadership competency can change over time and may even repeat itself. For example, let's say you'd like to become more influential in your approach with management, so you learn and practice listening skills. The result you receive from becoming a better listener may gain you the attention of senior management, ending in a promotion. Now ten years later, you are in the senior management job and you decide you need to fine-tune your influence skills for your executive role. The result from the same listening exercises may now lead to a more engaged and motivated team of employees because they feel valued and appreciated when you listen to their needs, ideas, and plans. So the reason changed for exercising and so did the result, even though the same exercise was repeated.

Whatever your reason for picking up this book or however you answer the Leadership Shape Self-Assessment, our hope is that you will get into leadership shape where you have lower scores on the assessment, and stay in leadership shape where you have high scores.

Feel free to explore through the chapters and work on the areas that need your attention most. The leadership exercises at the end of each competency chapter are designed to inspire you to act, leading to changed and effective leadership results. When followed start to finish, these exercises will indeed get you into leadership shape. In the stories ahead you will meet everyday leaders with pertinent examples to show you what this all looks like.

And if you take any of these to heart, and change your behavior, you will impact the people around you. Leaders with strong character competencies influence the marketplace, their communities, their inner circles, making the world a better place for all of us. That's a mighty good reason to exercise.

GETTING STARTED
People will evaluate you as a leader based on these three questions:

Can I trust you?
Are you committed to excellence?
Do you care about me?

As we begin the process of getting into leadership shape, let's first look at the role of leadership versus management. What is the difference between these two? We are often asked this question in training sessions and one-on-one coaching meetings.

A manager is a person who is in charge. There are managers for departments, projects, teams and companies. The manager holds responsibility for the details of the program, assignments, schedules, and agendas. Others work *for* the manager.

A leader is someone who inspires followers. Leaders aren't always formal managers. You can recognize them in the workplace, at church, at home, among your friends and just about everywhere you look. Leaders have *willing* followers—cohorts who aren't following solely because they are paid to do so. They follow because the leader has a meaningful cause, a purpose or vision worth attaching to, a talent that others want to learn, a belief in others' abilities to carry out a task or function, perhaps a natural gift of hope and encouragement.

So only managers who are good *leaders* will get ongoing results through a motivated and engaged team.

Frequently an organization will recognize the skills of a high performer and promote this individual into management. The new manager is placed in charge and given the responsibility of leading his team to productive results. The new manager knows he is more skilled than most of the people he is now managing. So what does he do? He shows his direct reports exactly how he wants the job done. He put controls and processes in place so that work is done his way. In his mind it's the *right* way. We call this the Quarterback Syndrome.

We were asked to coach a sales manager in the high-tech industry who had been promoted to this position because he was the best sales person in the company. He had expressed the desire for more challenge and responsibility, and the company wanted to keep him (and his customers).

As part of our coaching, we conducted a Leadership 360-Degree Assessment, an effective tool that creates awareness by interviewing coworkers. The assessment captured his team's perspective of his perceived strengths and weaknesses. We also implemented an additional behavioral assessment to measure his natural strengths and weaknesses as a technical sales manager in comparison to the rest of the US working population.

What both assessments suggested was while this was a very confident person who demonstrated high proficiency in task management, independence, self-motivation, energy, technical and sales skills, he was lacking two key things: 1) the ability to demonstrate a belief in his people and their individual styles for getting results, and 2) the ability to see himself as the new coach of the team rather than the star quarterback.

In our initial interview, we learned that this leader had been trying to lead for the previous eighteen months as the sales leader by telling his sales team how he, the expert, had become the number one sales person in the company. He had his team watch him in action. He went out on sales calls with his sales people, closing the sales for them to demonstrate how it should be done. He kept the top ten accounts for himself because, of course, only he could handle those customers. In addition, he put the kind of incentive programs in place that he found motivational rather than identifying incentives that would motivate his team.

While most of our coaching assignments turn into long-term, impactful behavior changes, it only took two one-on-one coaching meetings and a couple of assessments to reach a heart-to-heart conversation where this technical sales manager admitted he wasn't willing to learn to be the coach. The recognition of the top salesperson quarterback was what got him up every morning.

We worked with HR and the president to help this leader save face and identify a unique position that met everyone's needs and ultimately delivered results for the company.

Through the intensive assessment process that we use to identify natural leadership, we can predict with reliable accuracy the people who, with leadership development and training, will excel and sincerely enjoy their leadership role. However, if people do not have natural wiring or leadership DNA they can still excel greatly in a leadership role with proper coaching and leadership exercises. They may not enjoy the role as much as someone who is naturally wired for it, and they may also have a perspective that leading people is a lot of work, but if they are committed to getting into leadership shape, they can succeed.

So are leaders made or born? We believe the best leaders are born, *then* made. That's why the lessons and exercises in this book are so important. The eight competencies defined in this book are the most necessary developmental opportunities for any leader. These elements of leadership can be learned and exercised and put into practice, making you the leader you were born to be.

So, what is a leader? What has been proven to us over time is that the simplest way to define leadership is that good leaders **realize a vision through a belief in themselves and others**.

A good friend of ours and soon-to-be retiring CEO asked us to help him identify his successor among his four current Vice Presidents. He made it clear that he couldn't take the risk of losing the other three Vice Presidents once he promoted one of them to CEO, so he engaged us to accomplish this goal.

The plan that we developed included but was not limited to:

1. *An assessment to determine natural leadership ability and a leadership 360 survey to identify others' perception of their leadership.*

2. *Executive coaching and leadership development for the four candidates.*

3. *A strategic planning session that included strategic and tactical goals with all four VPs to set the future of the organization.*

4. *Four individual presentations and final business plans submitted to the CEO for evaluation of their ability to successfully lead this well-known "brand" name leader in their industry.*

In the third step, the strategic planning session, it became evident as to who the leader would be. The other three VPs were following only one leader in the meeting. They looked to him for the answers. They looked to him for decisions. The leader in the group was also the one asking the questions, the one they trusted, and the one who showed care and concern for the other three VPs as well as the employees, not just the projects.

It turns out that he was the one with the vision for the future of the company and the knowledge of the current financial situation. He was the one with the best leadership 360-degree feedback survey, which suggested he already had followers who believed in him. He was the one who had a well thought through business plan and presentation. And yes…he was the one who got the job.

So did the other VP's stay? Yes, they did, because they already saw their chosen colleague as their leader. Our evaluation and coaching process revealed his leadership to them, as well as to us and the existing CEO. What did this leader possess that set him apart? He had a vision for the company and a belief in himself and the other VPs to carry out the vision.

The key to success for any leader or manager, whether born for leadership or not, is the continued and relentless development and awareness of leadership skills. So let's get into leadership shape!

A good leader is:

- **Someone who has a vision,**
- **Someone his team can trust,**
- **Someone with a commitment to excellence,**
- **Someone who demonstrates belief in her people,**
- **And someone who cares about his people personally and professionally.**

SELF-ASSESSMENT
Getting Into Leadership Shape

This self-assessment will help you identify the leadership competencies that you naturally excel in as well as the competencies where improvement may be considered. The assessment will help you identify which chapters in this book to focus on first, next, and last based upon how you score.

Directions: In this self-assessment, please respond to each statement as accurately and honestly as possible by circling the number that best expresses the degree to which the statement is true for you. Circle a "5" if you would say the statement is "exactly like me" or a "1" if the statement is "not at all like me." You may also want to look at a "5" as something that you excel in and look at a "1" as something that is a weakness. Consider both your personal and professional life when completing this assessment. Also consider answering from someone's perspective who knows you well. You might start each question with "People who know me well would say…" *Place a check mark in the column next to the statement if this is an area in which you would like to improve.*

COURAGEOUS CONFIDENCE	Not Like Me	Exactly Like Me	✓
1. I can think of at least five to ten calculated risks that I have taken to improve my life and have evidence to show for it.	1 2 3	4 5	
2. I am genuinely very happy with my talents, abilities, and personality.	1 2 3	4 5	
3. I give myself room to make mistakes from which I can learn.	1 2 3	4 5	
4. I am comfortable with the risk associated with quick decisions.	1 2 3	4 5	
5. I am not concerned that people will judge me for my beliefs and actions.	1 2 3	4 5	

	Not Like Me	Exactly Like Me	✓
6. I am happy about the progress that I have made in life.	1 2 3 4 5		
7. I do not have a problem with worry, anxiety, or stress in my life.	1 2 3 4 5		
TOTAL POINTS:			

TRUST AND RESPECT	Not Like Me	Exactly Like Me	✓
1. People know me personally, because I am transparent and open with them about my personal and work life.	1 2 3 4 5		
2. I will avoid going "around others" to get a project done or my personal needs met.	1 2 3 4 5		
3. People come to me for opinions, ideas, and to discuss personal problems more than the average person.	1 2 3 4 5		
4. Others view me as a person who meets deadlines and follows-thru on commitments.	1 2 3 4 5		
5. I can honestly say that in the last year, I have not shared something that was supposed to be confidential.	1 2 3 4 5		
6. I avoid language that "shames others." Such as "You're not going to wear that/say that/do that, are you?"	1 2 3 4 5		
7. I avoid embarrassing or making fun of others.	1 2 3 4 5		
TOTAL POINTS:			

INTEGRITY	Not Like Me	Exactly Like Me	✓
1. I have communicated what is or isn't acceptable in terms of how people act or communicate around me.	1 2 3 4 5		
2. I know what I believe, and will defend my opinions.	1 2 3 4 5		
3. I am the same person at home as I am at work.	1 2 3 4 5		
4. My personal life values are written and I consider them when making life decisions.	1 2 3 4 5		
5. I have work-related values (expectations of behavior) and have communicated them, in writing, to the people I work with the most.	1 2 3 4 5		
6. People who know me well would say that I am honest in dealings with others.	1 2 3 4 5		
7. I am comfortable saying "no" to people or things that I don't trust, agree with, or believe in.	1 2 3 4 5		
TOTAL POINTS:			

COMMUNICATION AND CONFLICT	Not Like Me	Exactly Like Me	✓
1. I communicate in a respectful and straightforward manner, even when dealing with sensitive topics.	1 2 3 4 5		
2. I ask people for their opinions first before giving them mine.	1 2 3 4 5		
3. Before I take something that someone says or does personally, I go to them to confirm and clarify my understanding.	1 2 3 4 5		
4. I listen carefully, without interrupting.	1 2 3 4 5		
5. I am good at asking questions about the other person to keep conversations flowing.			
6. I can think of many times when I have given someone the "benefit of the doubt" rather than holding onto resentment.	1 2 3 4 5		

	Not Like Me	Exactly Like Me	✓
7. Others would say that I am good at expressing myself – my intentions, my ideas, and my feelings.	1 2 3	4 5	
TOTAL POINTS:			

ACCOUNTABILITY	Not Like Me	Exactly Like Me	✓
1. I accept responsibility for my mistakes without blaming other people or circumstances.	1 2 3	4 5	
2. I jump in and help rather than wait to be told what to do.	1 2 3	4 5	
3. I rarely solicit sympathy from others in order to make myself feel better.	1 2 3	4 5	
4. I have not broken any policies of the organization that I work for.	1 2 3	4 5	
5. I regularly reach out (verbally or in a survey) for feedback from others to see where there are opportunities for my improvement.	1 2 3	4 5	
6. I rarely let an obstacle or setback keep me from continuing the pursuit of a goal.	1 2 3	4 5	
7. When somebody has taken the blame for a problem I rightly caused, I immediately jump in and correct it.	1 2 3	4 5	
TOTAL POINTS:			

INFLUENCE	Not Like Me	Exactly Like Me	✓
1. People who know me well would say that I have a special ability to positively influence others.	1 2 3	4 5	
2. In the last week, I can think of something that I have done to appreciate someone.	1 2 3	4 5	
3. When someone approaches me with an emotional situation, I always listen, ask questions and demonstrate care and concern for that individual's feelings.	1 2 3	4 5	
4. I continuously train and educate people by giving experiences that help them adopt new attitudes and actions.	1 2 3	4 5	
5. I show genuine interest in others by asking them for their viewpoints and ideas before inserting mine.	1 2 3	4 5	
6. I share a contagious enthusiasm that promotes a positive attitude in others.	1 2 3	4 5	
7. I know the personal dreams, hobbies and interests of the top ten people that I interact or work with the most.	1 2 3	4 5	
TOTAL POINTS:			

FUTURE FOCUS	Not Like Me	Exactly Like Me	✓
1. I have a clear mission and purpose in life.	1 2 3	4 5	
2. I am internally driven and motivated to accomplish my personal and work goals.	1 2 3	4 5	
3. I assess "where I stand" today against "where I want to be" in the future at least once a year.	1 2 3	4 5	
4. I have a written action plan for the achievement of my goals.	1 2 3	4 5	
5. I have a written list or visual dream board that I use to motivate me.	1 2 3	4 5	

	Not Like Me	Exactly Like Me	✓
6. I look at things around me and I am able to envision how they can and will be better.		1 2 3 4 5	
7. I have a picture of the future that I am committed to fulfilling.		1 2 3 4 5	
TOTAL POINTS:			

DISCIPLINE	Not Like Me	Exactly Like Me	✓
1. I spend most of my time in activities that will get me to my goals.		1 2 3 4 5	
2. I have not lost my temper, yelled, or overtly lost control of my emotions anytime in the last six months.		1 2 3 4 5	
3. I collect enough data to make good decisions before I go ahead and decide.		1 2 3 4 5	
4. I make "appointments with myself" to do important tasks.		1 2 3 4 5	
5. In the last 6 months, I can think of an obstacle and/or frustration that I faced in which I demonstrated perseverance rather than surrendering to despair or giving up.		1 2 3 4 5	
6. I am self-disciplined in all areas of my life such as spending, eating, exercising, and emotions.		1 2 3 4 5	
7. I don't start things that I know I can't finish.		1 2 3 4 5	
TOTAL POINTS:			

Scoring and Evaluation

With the exception of those who have been through an incredible amount of self-assessment and awareness, our tendencies as human beings are to score ourselves higher on a self-evaluation than someone else may score us. Why? Because we tend to judge ourselves on the person we *intend* to be, not the person that other people see. Our suggestion is to meet with someone whom you know and trust to discuss the assessment and how you scored yourself. Let them know that you are looking for honest feedback. Then when they share something difficult, thank them for caring enough to tell you the truth.

Now, total your scores for each of the leadership competencies. A perfect score for each competency is 35 points. Any score of 28 points or higher would suggest that you are already an accomplished leader in that competency. This book will help you keep that competency in leadership shape. Scores lower than 28 points identify competencies that you'll want to examine and exercise. Regardless of your own self-perception, opportunities for improvement await you in this book.

THE 8 CORE CHARACTER COMPETENCIES FOR LEADERSHIP EFFECTIVENESS

Courageous Confidence

Trust and Respect

Integrity

Communication & Conflict

Accountability

Influence

Future Focus

Self-Discipline

Competency One
COURAGEOUS CONFIDENCE

In this Chapter, we will:

- Define confidence—why leaders have it in some areas and not in others.

- Discover the difference between self-image and self-esteem and the importance of these in leadership.

- Recognize the difference between arrogance and confidence while assessing yourself in these two areas.

- Learn how to develop the courage that motivates sensible risk-taking.

- Identify new strategies for managing fear and doubt.

- Give you exercises to improve your confidence.

Chapter One
COURAGEOUS CONFIDENCE

Are you making the move or controlling the fall?

A person who expects to lead others will have difficulty doing so without confidence. The world needs confident leaders who have a vision, can think beyond problems, and can courageously inspire people to convert challenges into opportunities. In fact, the true measure of leadership is in demonstrating the courage it takes to cross over into the less comfortable unknowns, and to *do it with confidence*. In this chapter, you will learn how to develop the courageous confidence required to be a true leader.

Confidence is a belief that you can succeed at something and will demonstrate it by taking action. When you are confident, you will take more risks because you believe in your talents and abilities to get the desired results. For instance, if I am confident that I can speak well in front of large groups, I will act upon that confidence and do so. I'll accept the keynote speaking engagement for the spring conference or volunteer to MC the awards dinner, confident in my potential to perform well. In contrast, if I lack confidence in public speaking, I will either avoid the podium at all cost or I will make excuses to explain my dismal failure in front of the microphone. In other words, because of my low confidence, I find ways to soften, or control, my inevitable fall.

The irony of confidence is that it can only develop in the realms of fear and the unknown, two dynamics that basic human nature works hard to avoid. Confidence grows when you take action and attempt challenges that are difficult and fearful, when you recognize a purpose and venture outside your comfort zone to accomplish it.

As a gymnast myself and an NCAA Women's Gymnastics coach, I (Ed) observed courageous confidence, and the lack of it, in many young athletes. In the sport of men's gymnastics, the high bar is a very intimidating event because of its high level of danger. One particular move on high bar is called a Kovac, a flying backflip above a nine-foot high apparatus. The gymnast lets go of the bar, does a backflip over the top and then re-grabs the bar on the way down. The risk of injury is huge.

To make the move, the gymnast needs to add power, release longer, and go higher, but when young athletes lack confidence in accomplishing the move, they try to control their fall by releasing too quickly and not adding enough power. They think that if they don't go as high, they won't get hurt as badly if they miss the re-grab on the way back down. This puts the gymnast out of position and inevitably results in a fall, occasionally resulting in a trip to the emergency room. The vision of the potential damage takes on greater meaning than the accomplishment of the move, at which point the goal becomes to control one's fall.

One time I was coaching a young girl who asked me to spot her on a scary dismount on the women's uneven bars. I noticed that she was dragging a six-inch pad to help cushion the already existing four-inch pad under the high bar.

"What's that for?" I asked her.

She looked at me with fear in her eyes and replied, "What if I fall?"

I instantly recognized her lack of confidence. She was focused on the consequences of crashing, not the exhilaration of making the necessary moves to be successful.

"Well," I answered, "what if you do the series of events that it takes to make the move, what do you think will happen? Do you think that you will need the crash pad?"

She responded, "I'll make the move."

"Then just do that instead," I encouraged. But she was unwilling to attempt the move without the extra crash pads.

So on this particular day, I sent her to the locker room and told her that once she was ready to make the move, I would spot her.

You see, when a person lacks confidence, she will put more focus into controlling the fall than in making the move. Her fear will cause her to put "crash pads" in place... just in case. But *controlling the fall* will never produce the same success, the exhilaration and self-fulfillment as *making the move* to pursue and overcome an intimidating task. Both require effort, but only one will actually make the move and help build confidence. Only doing the full series of events it takes to make the move will actually make the move. Anything less, and you are controlling the fall, so you put crash pads under yourself for damage control… just in case.

Leaders telegraph if they're focused on making the move or controlling the fall whether they know it or not.

A few years ago, we were conducting a strategic planning meeting with a senior leadership team of nine members. The owner of the company was well respected and loved by his employees. He had built the company to a successful sixty-million dollar company and wanted our guidance to help him take it to 100 million.

We had just spent two and a half days identifying the company's strengths, weaknesses, opportunities, and threats, and had identified long-range and short-range goals. The team was excited about putting the strategies in place.

The first problem arose when we started working on roles, responsibilities, and decision-making authority. We asked each team member to identify 1) the decisions they had ultimate authority to make without input from others, 2) the decisions they were responsible for making but only after getting input from other team members, and 3) the decisions that they would like to have more input in making. After the team members shared their responses, we asked the CEO and owner for his decision-making authority.

"I don't think that I should ever make any decisions without checking in first with my team," he revealed. He respected others' opinions and wanted them to know their voices were heard.

But we also sensed there was a possibility that he sometimes feared he would upset one of his executives, causing the executive to leave the company.

One brave member of the team at this point spoke up. "Respectfully, sir, that's a huge problem for us. We can't seem to make decisions fast enough here. Everything has to go to a committee. And the nine of us all have differing opinions causing us to stall and miss opportunities that come our way. Sometimes, what we need you to do is just make the decision knowing that you won't please 100% of us."

And this executive was right. The owner was controlling the fall by using the "I will get agreement from everyone first" crash pad to avoid making tough choices. So the owner agreed that he would start making a few bolder decisions more often rather than trying to accommodate everyone.

About two hours later he was tested. A tough decision needed to be made that two of the executives were not in favor of moving forward on. The owner was having difficulty making the decision, knowing that it might make two key executives unhappy.

We reminded the owner of his crash pad and his opportunity here to make the move, so he made the decision to move forward. Then we went around the room and asked the team if they would now support the owner in this decision. After all, we recapped, they wanted to see him "put his foot down more often and make the decision, right?"

When we asked the two "hold-outs" for their support, their answers were "yes, we will support him but we have a few questions first." Terrific! This is how communication should happen. The owner answered their questions and all were in agreement to move forward.

The owner told us later that he learned a valuable lesson. For years he had relied on two other business partners to give him the confidence to make tough decisions, and now that he was the only partner left, and head of the company, this was uncomfortable. But it was also holding the team back. The owner's crash pads of requiring approval from every executive before making decisions had been negatively impacting the whole company.

We have witnessed a variety of "crash pads" from low confidence people over the years. You too may be putting crash pads in your life to avoid the fear of failing or the possibility of embarrassment, or to keep a particular weakness private. See if you can recognize yourself in any of the examples below.

Crash pads may look like:

1. The *"staying in control"* crash pad:

    To stay in control, you will quit your job before you are fired. You may be afraid that you are going to get written up, scolded, or fired, so you resign first. You'd rather quit your job than deal with the negative consequences. At least you're in control, you may justify. Or, as a leader, you micromanage your team because it makes you feel like you are in control. Most often this is your fear taking charge, not your team's lack of competence. Another term for "micromanagement" is "lack of trust and communication." It's a crash pad.

2. The *"avoiding embarrassment"* crash pad:

   This pad shows up at a very early childhood age. For example, as a child you tell someone you like that you are not interested in being friends because you are afraid he or she is not interested in you. When this long-rooted behavior resurfaces in adulthood, a leader chooses a less-qualified employee to lead a project rather than assigning the task to a more competent staff member, afraid the smarter candidate might make the leader look inferior.

3. The *"avoiding risk"* crash pad:

   Your small business is at a crossroads, and your financial advisor informs you your accounts are running low. Rather than allowing the possibility of failure, you cut back on business expenses instead of spending money to grow the business. Or it may be as simple as avoiding a conversation with your boss about how bored you are in your job in the event she gives you other work that you don't like, or worse, gets you fired.

4. The *"lowering your standard"* crash pad:

   Individuals who lower their standards in an effort to gain acceptance do not see themselves worthy of respect. Tragically, this may happen when you choose a mate with many flaws because you don't feel you're worthy enough to attract the better person. Leaders often mistakenly lower their standards thinking it inspires acceptance. For example, in an effort to show how flexible she is, the Customer Service Manager may tell her team that she doesn't care what hours they work as long as they give her forty hours a week. Her employees take advantage of her reckless policy, and customer satisfaction scores go down because the phones are not adequately staffed.

5. The *"prevent disappointment"* crash pad:

    You buy only one ticket to the concert just in case you can't find anyone to go with you. In fact, you believe you will probably be attending the concert alone anyway, so why even try to find someone to go with you. A leadership team can put this crash pad under an entire organization by setting goals too low or reducing production numbers. Unfortunately, in their effort to prevent disappointment, they infuse an over-cautious reluctance to perform into the workplace culture.

6. The *"evading the truth"* crash pad:

    When you receive a negative performance appraisal you bad-mouth the appraisal process or your boss to a coworker, instead of looking at how you can improve your performance so that you minimize damage should you get the same review next year.

7. The *"avoid conflict"* crash pad:

    Rather than having a conversation with your spouse that you are miserable and unhappy in your marriage and that you want to go to marriage counseling, you instead stay miserable and become difficult to live with. At work, you'd rather change your work schedule than continue working with a difficult coworker. Leaders may avoid giving a boss or an employee direct and honest feedback, concerned it will make the person feel bad.

8. The *"fear of judgment"* crash pad:

    You hesitate to invite friends over for dinner because you are concerned they may judge your house or your housekeeping skills. Leaders double-up and triple-up this crash pad with the *"avoiding risk"* crash pad and the *"avoiding embarrassment"* crash pad. Now nothing gets done.

9. The *"comfort zone"* crash pad:

    Given two options—1) remain in your current home or job where you are comfortable and life is relatively easy, or 2) move your family across the country to be with family and friends whom you cherish—you stay put. Perhaps you don't accept a new job or position within the company because you view change as uncomfortable and not exhilarating.

10. The *"needing to be liked"* crash pad:

    As a teen with this crash pad in place, you go with your friends to a party where drugs and alcohol will be flowing, instead of telling your friends that you do not want to open yourself up to those kinds of temptations. As an adult, you spend the first twenty minutes of a meeting telling jokes when the time would be better off spent on a business subject.

11. The *"need to fit in"* crash pad:

    You join a group conversation that includes bad-mouthing a friend or coworker instead of defending the person by helping your friends see him from a different perspective.

12. The *"need to be politically correct"* crash pad:

    You do not share your personal opinion or spiritual beliefs with a friend for fear your ideas are not politically correct. Or due to the politics played out in the workplace, you remain silent when your boss considers a decision you strongly disagree with because it is not politically correct to question the boss.

We have all set up crash pads to control our fall, in one way or another. Everyone has a personal set of fears. Some are simple and some become quite complicated, but they all end up with the same result—an inhibition to move forward.

Sometimes we fear because we doubt that we have control over something, so we continue to harbor doubt until doubting becomes a habitual way of responding to the risk or fear, and before we know it the crash pads are stacked ever higher. But controlling the fall will never, *ever*, make the move necessary to reach our desired outcome.

I (Janet) am a frequent flyer even though I am afraid of flying. I would much rather put in the crash pad of driving to wherever I need to get to. But that is not efficient or reasonable in most cases, so I choose to seize the opportunity to overcome my fear by booking flights whenever possible. The good news is that we can decide to get rid of the crash pads in our lives and free ourselves to make the first move, no matter how daunting that may seem.

Just be sure to not get stuck on the first move.

It is a common practice in gymnastics to approach the more difficult moves by practicing what's known as a "timer." A timer is essentially the first part of a move. It allows the gymnast to understand the timing necessary to enter into the full move. However, if not careful, with continual repetition the timer can eventually become the mistaken goal. Gymnasts have been known to practice timers for months, causing the timer to become an excuse for not executing the full move.

The caution is to not get in the habit of practicing leadership timers as an excuse to avoid the fear of the full leadership move.

One's fears can be embarrassing in the work environment, so people take great measures to mask them by double and triple stacking their crash pads. Since leaders often connect fear to weakness, that in turn leads to a fear of being judged. So they put a crash pad in place to mask them. For example, a leader may have a fear or belief that he has poor boardroom or presentation skills. Rather than admitting his weakness and getting the coaching he needs to develop this weak area, he cancels meetings and makes excuses for being late to presentations, avoiding his obligations out of fear he might look foolish. This is a selfish behavior and puts the individual's interest ahead of that of the organization. Fears are so personal and so emotional that they take on an amazing reality.

Everyone has a basic fear of the unknown, which causes a natural resistance to change or risk. Moving forward in life will, with certainty, come with encounters of fear. But it is crucial to decipher the difference between real obstacles and imagined ones. And when you face fear with the determination to not let it stifle your dreams, fear can become a positive motivator. Once you defy the anxiety ahead of you, you can prepare for action to overcome the danger, whether perceived or real.

Notice how two people can have the same fear, yet that fear stifles one person and not the other. Why is one inspired to tap inner courage and not the other? Perhaps the answer is revealed in a quote by Bethany Hamilton, the well-known female surfer who had her left arm ripped off in a shark attack, yet continued to be victorious in her competitive surfing career. She connected the missing thought that is absolutely critical in overcoming fear when she said, *"My passion for surfing was more than my fear of sharks."* Focusing on your passion, your goal, will stir your courage to manage your fear.

So what can you do to overcome fear? First of all, make the decision to move ahead. You can dispel fear by:

1. Gathering facts,
2. Evaluating them, and
3. Recognizing and embracing the fact that decisions must ordinarily be made on the basis of partial data. Have the mindset to know that not all components of the move can be known at the beginning. You will learn parts of the move in the middle of the move, and handle unforeseen obstacles as they present themselves.

When you follow these steps, fear loses its hold and all of the reasons why you thought you shouldn't or can't or won't make the move all become irrelevant. When you see that making a move requires

> **Pushing through fear is a decision, not a skill. Once you recognize this important truth, you realize you can acquire the skill or obtain the resources necessary to accomplish your goal.**

a particular skill or resource, notice how you are always one skill or one resource short of beginning. When you decide to "make the move" and it is executed successfully, what once was a fear is now a self-satisfying, confidence-boosting exhilaration.

There are a couple of basic premises that need to be accepted as a normal aspect of making any move. First, executing any significant move for the first time is not normal, so accept that. Doing a backflip over the high bar twelve feet off the ground for the very first time is not normal, but not normal does not translate to not achievable. Once the habit is formed, any move that seemed foreign at the beginning becomes normal. So give yourself time and space to form the habit. Secondly, understand that part of learning and understanding any worthwhile move is learned somewhere in the middle of the move. Don't think you have to understand every aspect of a challenge to enter into it. In the beginning, it is better to rely more on courage and less on understanding.

Courage is one response human nature can rely on to manage fear. But we as a society have been conditioned to associate fear with cowardice. That implies that the courageous person is never afraid, which is simply not true. It would be more accurate to interpret that statement to mean that the confident and courageous person is not dominated by fears. A brave person removes crash pads, and uses fears constructively to do something about the dangers that threaten the goal.

For example, if you desire to learn a foreign language and you study, practice, and even perhaps embarrass yourself when attempting dialogue, bit-by-bit you will become more confident in your abilities. You may never be perfect, but that's not the point. Confidence is about facing obstacles and realizing that your confidence has grown, even when you fail.

And let's face it… some moves are easier to make than others, for all of us. Psychologists consider confidence to be domain specific. In other words, it is both possible and normal to be confident in one area of your life, but lack any semblance of confidence in another. I may be confident that I am a good parent but think I am a horrible boss, for example. Or, an executive may harbor little fear in a board-room but is deathly terrified in a courtroom. An explorer may find exploring the unknowns of the jungle to be super exhilarating but is very fearful in a relationship. A leader in the organization may be comfortable with public speaking, but is fearful when called to be transparent.

The challenge with developing confidence is that it is intertwined with a person's self-esteem and self-image. The higher your self-esteem, the better chance of confidence. From early childhood on, you began to make associations and draw conclusions based upon your environment and how you related to it, particularly through your interactions with others. We all form attitudes, perceptions, and beliefs at a young age that limit our actions. For example, the "Go home! I don't want to play with you" reaction you may have suffered from your peers on the schoolyard may have played a role in the way you learned to view the world around you, and more importantly, how you viewed your place in it.

Fathers, mothers, older siblings, and teachers all have an influence on us during our childhood. You may have heard it said that children have certain traits of their parents. If they do, it is typically not because they inherited these traits, but because they were conditioned; they *learned* the specific traits. Not only by example or by actions relevant to us that were taken or not taken, but by words – advice, arguments, or persuasion – we form an idea of what to expect of ourselves. Some family influence encourages people to try a little harder, to be better, more successful and to achieve greater things than anyone else in their family. Conversely, family influence may convince others that they can never match the achievements of a father, mother, or older sibling, severely handicapping an individual's self-esteem and self-image.

The difference between self-esteem and self-image is simply this: Self-esteem is what *you* think of yourself. Self-image is what you believe *others* think of you. For example, if a human being lived within a cave and never interacted with another person, would she ever desire plastic surgery? Likely not, because it is in the presence and interaction with other people that the inadequacy of this image reveals itself. Yet, the opinions of others matter little when a person has a healthy, and confident, self-esteem.

As you age through life, there are many factors that play on your ability to maintain a healthy confidence, self-image and self-esteem. These factors are both external and internal. Positive experiences (i.e. your successes) affect the way in which you view yourself by bolstering your self-esteem. On the other hand, negative experiences (i.e. your failures) can lower self-esteem and confidence, stifling your ability to try new things. Your self-esteem can evolve up or down, without any conscious direction. It is never static, because of life's inevitable failures and successes.

We often perceive the opinions that others have about us, both good and bad, as an authentic reflection of ourselves. It doesn't matter whether our perception is accurate or not. It's the way we tend to think about ourselves that is determinant of the roles we assume, the goals we set, and the successes we achieve. Family influences, like business and social influences should always be weighed in the balance of our own values, needs and desires, and subjected to our own freedom of choice.

You may not intentionally decide to have a positive self-esteem or negative self-esteem, and you may find yourself appreciating some of your talents and abilities, and hating other flaws about yourself. Or you may think you don't have many, if any, flaws at all.

Confidence is Not Arrogance

People often associate confidence with arrogance, but they are distinctly different. Before we talk about that difference, answer the following questions to determine if you are confident or arrogant. But be forewarned… arrogance is inherently dishonest. Arrogant people don't see their own arrogance as a bad thing. They often justify it as confidence, but we will show how arrogance is definitely not confidence and that it is destructive.

Be honest with yourself as you answer the following questions and think about how others would rate you.

1. When you read a leadership book authored by a famous leader like Jack Welch, do you read to learn, or read to see how your beliefs and perspectives so closely compare because it demonstrates how smart you already are?
2. When at a social function, are you constantly looking around the room for someone more influential to talk to rather than engaging in the conversation in front of you? Arrogant people try to maximize their worth by minimizing the worth of others. The consequence of this may result in a lack of trust and respect for the arrogant person. Confident people look you in the eyes and make you feel as though you are the most important person in the room regardless of position or title.
3. Do you "name drop" in order to let others know who you pal around with, or as an attempt to "one-up" someone? Bragging is most often a form of deflection or masks a weakness, and confident people don't feel the need to brag. The consequence of bragging is that it minimizes the other person's value.
4. Are you consistently late to meetings…and don't apologize? Arrogant leaders have no need to apologize because to them their time is much more valuable than yours so an apology is not necessary. This can result in poor morale, fractured teams, and lack of engagement. Confident people recognize the importance of other people's time.
5. When in conversation with others, do you frequently interrupt

others? Arrogant leaders believe that they are smarter so there is no value for them in listening to you. The consequence is that this builds resentment and leads to disrespect. Confident people respect and listen to what others have to say.

6. Do you occasionally bad-mouth or put others down? Arrogant leaders feel the need to spread rumors because their worth shows up in the superiority they feel over others. The consequence of spreading rumors is that others will stop coming to you with information, which in turn leads to the arrogant leader making decisions without all the facts. Confident people are energized by the strengths in others. They don't listen to gossip fanatics who set up criticism with "I don't mean to spread rumors but...."

If you answered "yes" to more than one question listed above, others may see you as arrogant. Many leaders think that they are confident when in reality they are arrogant, stubborn and proud.

High confidence results in high performance. High arrogance does not necessarily result in high performance but when it does, there is often collateral damage as a consequence. In the arrogant pursuit of a goal, other people get hurt.

You've seen the difference! The arrogant leader is someone who suffers from an over-inflated ego, sometimes a cover-up for an inferior self-esteem. Arrogant leaders can come across as bullies, taking credit for other people's successes and blaming others for their failures. Their decisions are driven by what will make them look good and what will gain them the most.

Confident leaders have an internal connection to their competence and sense of worth, driven by a mindset of humility. Arrogant leaders see their worth as it compares to somebody else so their worth doesn't reveal itself until they can demonstrate superiority driven by righteousness. Confident leaders pursue knowledge for clarity. Arrogant leaders pursue knowledge to prove they are right and you're wrong.

Remember, it takes confidence to lead, but it takes humility for the leader to be followed. Humility involves a stance that is others-oriented instead of self-focused. And only a person with healthy self-esteem can live that way.

Self-esteem is the value you see yourself having in the world. "Am I a worthwhile human being with talents, abilities, and a good personality?" Answer that question with a "yes" and chances are you have healthy self-esteem. This idea may seem simple, but it is reasonable. Let's take a look at how this plays out as a leader in the workplace.

Someone who is in charge of leading a group of people will only lead as effectively as his confidence allows and what's more detrimental, typically hires people only to the level of his own courage and confidence. For example, if I have a healthy self-esteem and believe in my talents, I may volunteer for more projects, make quicker decisions, feel deserving of happiness, and enter into an endeavor without needing to know everything about it. I am not as severely impacted by conflict and discouragements. This often gets me noticed and promoted by management. I become someone others put their confidence in.

But imagine I am a manager with low self-esteem who is in charge of projects and people. I don't take action or make decisions quickly enough, resulting in missed opportunities. I don't volunteer my department for a high profile project. I limit my employees' opportunities to learn new systems because I'm not confident I can lead my team to success.

A manager or leader who has low self-esteem is not confident hiring people with higher self-esteem. These managers hire employees only up to their level of self-esteem, thereby limiting the productivity of an entire department. A manager who discounts his talents, abilities, and personality often fears that others more confident will make him look stupid, inept, or ineffective. So subconsciously he resorts to hiring lower self-esteemed employees who are also fearful or covered in doubt, thereby getting mediocre results.

Unlike the less-confident leader, the confident leader recognizes and is comfortable with the collective talents and high confidence of his people, thereby relinquishing control to the team instead of restricting it out of fear of losing control and self-worth.

People follow leaders who understand their strengths and weaknesses and embrace them with all they are worth. People follow leaders who recognize opportunities for improvement, and who don't beat themselves up when they don't have a natural talent that someone else on the team may possess. Confident leaders don't give concern to such things. They focus on developing their self-esteem so that they are comfortable hiring people who are confident. This will lead to a more productive life, department, and/or company.

Developing Courageous Confidence

So all of this leads to the point about how to develop courageous confidence. While environment (past and present) plays a critical role in the way you see yourself in relation to the world around you, it is possible to take control of your way of thinking and make a conscious decision to positively change your internal awareness of self, in other words improve your self-esteem, regardless of environmental factors or influences. Study the lives of Abraham Lincoln, Beethoven, Martin Luther King, Steve Jobs and many other successful people who made something incredible of their lives even though they came from the humblest of beginnings and had been told to quit wasting their time. You would see that external pressure (lack of finances, people skills, social status, etc.), alone cannot paint you with a self-esteem that becomes your absolute destiny. In fact, inherent in external pressures are often the opportunities to overcome challenges, demonstrate courage, and build self-esteem.

What we have learned we can unlearn, given a solid reason and a better environment. A personality that has been shaped by daily exposure to negativism can be reshaped by daily exposure to more positive influences.

If you want to have success in life (no matter how you personally define it), you will need to identify the belief system consistent with your definition of success and identify the actions you will need to take to get there. A belief system is your personal understanding of what is right or wrong, good or bad, productive or detrimental. For most of us, we need to change what we think, or else we won't find the motivation to act.

For example, if I want to become a good leader, I have to believe that *good leadership is made, not just born.* I have to believe that leadership is achievable and that the future payoff is worthy of effort today. Developing leadership requires observing and learning the behaviors that align with good leadership. If you learn and believe that good leadership of others means spending one-on-one time with each of your direct reports at least once a week, then you are more apt to strive to put that in your week, thus leading to the possibility that you are doing a better job of leading. If you don't believe it or your belief is weak, there is no purpose to the action and it won't get done.

Belief is the core driver of willingness, so if you want to be a pro at anything, it starts by believing that you can be. If you are not willing to take certain risks and actions, it will limit your success. If you are willing to take the appropriate actions because you believe you are worthy and that you can, then you will be willing to take the action that leads to success.

The problem is that our *habits of thought* get in the way of taking action.

> *I (Janet) wanted to be a sales and leadership trainer and develop my own entire course curriculum, but I was worried that I would not be as good as others. My lack of belief held me back for years.*
>
> *Even after I stepped out of my comfort zone and got over the fear of speaking in front of groups, I still didn't think that I could be a good enough writer. Then, in an effort to improve myself as a business leader, I joined a CEO roundtable group made up of powerful executives. There were a couple of CEOs in that group who believed in me, ahead of my belief in myself, and regularly encouraged me to develop the training material. Their premise was that I would make more money by having my own curriculum as well as more leverage when selling my company someday.*
>
> *Over time my habits of thought became conditioned through the repetition of hearing from a few CEOs who really cared about my success.*
>
> *As my perception of myself grew and strengthened as a writer and subject matter expert, my belief grew with it and I ventured out of my comfort zone and tried it. With my newly budding courage, I succeeded in writing my own curriculum. It catapulted my business and my confidence.*

What if you don't have positive feedback to help you retrain your habits of thought and develop confidence? That's where the exercises in this book come in to play. There is nothing that builds belief and confidence faster than mini-successes. Our exercises will help you build your confidence strength.

If you focus on *making the move* in the leadership role rather than *controlling the fall*, rewards are going to come much more quickly. Remember, confidence is the action or belief that you can do something. When embarking on something new, it takes boldness, courage, and belief that there will be a good result. Courage and confidence will prepare you so that when the opportunity presents itself, you will confidently say, "I can and I will." When you make the move and succeed, it is the most thrilling and confidence boosting thing that you can do for yourself, and your business. When looking back on your life, you will be able to see the accomplishments that made a difference for not only yourself, but for others as well. Especially when you did it all without crash pads.

ADVICE FROM YOUR COACH

When faced with tough decisions, ask yourself, "Am I making the move or controlling the fall?" Only by making the move and realizing the success of your decision will you achieve courageous confidence.
So, go make the move!

LEADERSHIP EXERCISES
COURAGEOUS CONFIDENCE

Leadership Exercise #1: CRASH PADS

Exercise Purpose: To remove negative behaviors caused by the fear of "making the move."

Expected Outcome: To be able to achieve more goals because your focus is more on the goal and the steps it takes to get there, rather than the crash pads in case you fall. Also, to develop an awareness of when you put crash pads in place, what they look like, why they are there, and how to not let them take the place of achieving the goal. This exercise will help you to admit the brutally honest truths about yourself and help you to identify your fears and related crash pads so that you can remove them. Be aware that crash pads and fears are different. Fear is a perceived outcome. A crash pad is a mechanism, an activity, a mindset that controls the fall, making the fall safer but sabotaging the goal.

Example: Before you begin filling out the Crash Pad Chart on the following page, here is an explanation with examples of how to fill out the Chart:

FEARS	CRASH PAD (Just in case I fail)	REASONS TO OVERCOME FEARS	SERIES OF EVENTS TO MAKE THE MOVE
Example: **Public Speaking**	*I will minimize the content value by letting everyone know that "**I didn't have time to prepare.**"*	*Develop confidence and build competence*	• *Get Prepared* • *Make the content rich* • *Practice* • *Get feedback before I deliver*

The fear of public speaking: Josh has a fear of public speaking. He has been asked by the company leadership to give a presentation at the annual meeting on a new product his team developed that resulted in a profitable company patent. Josh is deathly worried that his presentation will not meet expectations by the company or the audience, or that he will come across as an idiot, so he starts to contrive crash pads in his head that he will land on to explain why the presentation failed when the moment comes. These crash pads look like:

> **I didn't have time to prepare** crash pad – Meaning, "I knew it wasn't good, just like you probably thought. I'm aware of it, I know it, but I didn't have time to really prepare an exciting presentation." This crash pad is driven by Josh's real fear of failing at public speaking and catches Josh with excuses when he falls.

Josh is focused on the fear of failure. He can overcome this fear by identifying the reasons to engage in the presentation that are more important than the fear. The fear may seem real and big, but the reasons to engage in the fear are more meaningful than the fear itself. The possible reasons may include:

- People can sell the new product with greater vigor if they know the multitude of efforts implemented in developing the product. The company makes more money.
- Investors are more likely to invest with a higher confidence in the brain trust of the development team and a proven process to commercialize an idea.
- Josh is proud of the team accomplishments and can transfer that pride into the culture of the organization. Other people will feel good, proud, accomplished, recognized, and confident.

These reasons are so noble they reduce the fear from a barrier to a mere thought not worth stopping for.

What are the series of events it takes to deliver a successful speech (make the move)?

- Event #1 - Prepare: Determine what people want to hear. Find out what ideas management wants to convey. Find out what information the salespeople need to sell. Find out what drives an investor. Connect the product and the development process to ensure a homerun presentation.
- Event #2 - Determine the big ideas or key points: Establish the big ideas such as collaboration, problem solving, dedication to a goal, the company's ability to realize a vision. This will develop the belief Josh needs to speak with confidence and conviction.
- Event #3 - Practice: Thoroughly practice the belief as well as the actual speech.
- Event #4 - Get feedback on the speech ahead of the live event from several advisors to determine if the ideas are effectively conveyed.

If Josh leaves out any event, he is now controlling the fall. If Josh avoids getting feedback because he views it as wasting somebody's time or it's embarrassing, then he empowers the need for a crash pad and will likely put one in place. If Josh dedicates himself to each event it takes to make the move, the only outcome is achieving the goal of a successful speech at the annual company meeting.

On the following page, add your fears, identifiable crash pads, reasons and actions that you will take instead to "make the move."

FEARS	CRASH PAD (Just in case I fail)	REASONS TO OVERCOME FEARS	SERIES OF EVENTS TO MAKE THE MOVE
Example: *Spend the money to add an experienced sales person to the staff.*	*Hire a college kid instead and teach him/her to sell so that there is less money spent.*	*Grow the organi-zation and increase revenues*	• *Identify needed competencies* • *Advertise for position* • *Hire the most qualified*

LEADERSHIP EXERCISES
COURAGEOUS CONFIDENCE

Leadership Exercise #2: CONDITIONING IMPACT

Exercise Purpose: To establish an effective leadership attitude through positive conditioning.

We have conditioned influences (attitudes and actions) that come from four specific areas – family, social, work, and personal experiences of failures and mistakes. The purpose of this exercise is to identify your positive and negative conditioning, so as a leader you can identify the areas that are contributing to your success or holding you back from success.

Expected Outcome: To become aware of the actions and perceptions you derive from your positive and negative conditioning so these conditioning effects can be effectively managed. Positive conditioning can be leveraged with greater intention, and negative conditioning noticed and overcome so that it does not impact yourself or others negatively.

Example: Before you begin filling out the Conditioning Chart on the following page, here is an explanation with examples of how to fill out the Conditioning Chart:

AREA OF LIFE	POSITIVE CONDITIONING	POSITIVE IMPACT	NEGATIVE CONDITIONING	NEGATIVE IMPACT
Work	*I have been told throughout my career that "I am very organized."*	*My work environment is very clean and I always meet project deadlines.*	*I have been told that I should never manage people because I am not assertive enough nor do I speak up enough and offer ideas in meetings.*	*A belief that I'm not worth promoting therefore I don't pursue promotions.*

A change in thinking or action that I would like to make:
Work with my manager to create a development plan that includes assertiveness training and give him permission to hold me accountable.

Looking at these four areas, write down in the space below how were you conditioned positively (that have produced good results in your life) and negatively (that have led to negative results):

AREA OF LIFE	POSITIVE CONDITIONING	POSITIVE IMPACT	NEGATIVE CONDITIONING	NEGATIVE IMPACT
Work				

A change in thinking or action that I would like to make:

AREA OF LIFE	POSITIVE CONDITIONING	POSITIVE IMPACT	NEGATIVE CONDITIONING	NEGATIVE IMPACT
Social				

A change in thinking or action that I would like to make:

AREA OF LIFE	POSITIVE CONDITIONING	POSITIVE IMPACT	NEGATIVE CONDITIONING	NEGATIVE IMPACT
Family				

A change in thinking or action that I would like to make:

AREA OF LIFE	POSITIVE CONDITIONING	POSITIVE IMPACT	NEGATIVE CONDITIONING	NEGATIVE IMPACT
Past Mistakes				

A change in thinking or action that I would like to make:

Experiences of all kinds add to your self-confidence. List below the events that have added to your self-confidence:

EXPERIENCE	EVENT
A challenging goal that you have achieved	
A fear that you have overcome	
An award or recognition that you have received	
Something that you have learned to do	
A habit that you have developed	
A problem that you have solved	
An obstacle that you have overcome	
A friend you have helped	

Competency Two
TRUST AND RESPECT

In this Chapter, we will:

- Review the differences between trust and respect.

- Bring awareness to the four types of false leadership styles that when used by the leader cause others to lose respect rather than gain it.

- Discuss the strategies that lead to improved trust and respect.

- Show how demonstrating vulnerability and transparency is a way to improve trust.

- Practice how to be more direct in your communication as a way to build trust and respect.

- Give you a Trust and Respect questionnaire that you can use as a self-evaluation or give to someone else to help you evaluate whether people trust and respect you.

Chapter Two
TRUST AND RESPECT

We usually judge other people based upon their actions, but tend to judge ourselves based upon our intentions. How would your life look different if you reversed these two?

Is it possible to respect someone you don't trust, or to trust someone you don't respect? We think that it is possible, but not always probable. Before you make up your mind, let's take a closer look at both trust and respect.

The Merriam-Webster English dictionary defines trust as "assured reliance on the character, ability, strength, or truth of someone or something." Simply put, trust means assurance that the actions of others are consistent with their words.

Trust is the foundation upon which all relationships are built. It is central to stable and productive workplace relationships, teamwork, friendships, and marriages. High trust environments correlate positively with a high degree of commitment, involvement, team and organizational success.

There are two main types of trust, and they are both equally important. They are:

- Trust in the *competence of another* – that they have the skills, knowledge, and ability to carry out commitments necessary for personal and professional success.
- Trust in *the intentions of another* – that their words and deeds match up and that they will not take advantage of another person for personal gain or satisfaction.

In order to trust someone at work, you must be able to trust his ability to perform his job and meet deliverables, but you also have to trust that he "has your back." One without the other, and you won't truly be able to trust your coworker.

Douglas McGregor describes the importance of trust in his book *The Professional Manager.* "Trust means 'I know that you will not, deliberately or accidentally, consciously or unconsciously, take unfair advantage of me.' It means 'I can put my situation at the moment, my status and self-esteem in the group, our relationship, my job, my career, even my life in your hands with complete confidence.'" Trust in the workplace means that you have the assurance a person you work for, or with, is concerned about your welfare and interests apart from what you can do for him. And that the skills you have developed are valued by your manager, coworkers and the larger organization.

Respect, on the other hand, is a feeling of deep admiration for someone or something elicited by their abilities, qualities, or achievements. Respect has a lot to do with *competence* and *care*. One's achievements demonstrate their competence. Character qualities such as caring are demonstrated by asking questions and listening to others' opinions.

> *I (Janet) will never forget the time that I was in the president's office of one of my vendors when Paul J. Meyer walked in. Mr. Meyer (now deceased), founded and operated over forty companies, from real estate investments to jet leasing, and was well known as an authority in personal and professional development. I had never met him, but had heard a great deal about him and respected him for his many accomplishments.*
>
> *We were introduced and Paul immediately started asking me questions about my business and myself. He wanted to know my opinions and thoughts. He gave me a few tips on how to grow my business and asked me for my business card.*
>
> *A few weeks later, I received a quick little note from Paul to let me know that he enjoyed our conversation. Just a couple of sentences, but I respected him even more for taking the time to care.*

To earn someone's respect for you as a leader, you must demonstrate leadership qualities that are considered, well, respectable. Although it seems backwards, in order to be respected, you have to first respect others in the role they fill. You do that by accepting people as they are, by demonstrating respect regardless of your agreement with who they are and how they display opposing values.

Let's take a look at how a difference in values between two people commonly plays out in the workforce every day. Assertive people, as imagined, are often driven by a value of honesty, truthfulness, and transparency. Some behaviors of assertiveness are commonly viewed as taking charge, talking forcefully and often, speaking their mind, and quickly entering into conflict. They see their own assertiveness as a demonstration of competence and honesty, so when they are interacting with low assertive people who are not forceful and not automatically taking charge, they can mistakenly view them as lacking competence and honesty.

This perspective is often accompanied with a lack of trust and respect for the lower assertiveness. The lesson here is if you are naturally a low assertive person, you can earn trust and respect by demonstrating assertive behaviors while in the presence of assertive personalities. The moment might call for it. And if you are naturally highly assertive, trust and respect can be earned with lower assertive people by being a better listener, talking less, and encouraging other people to share their opinions. Assertiveness like every behavior is effective at the right time and in the right proportion to achieve a desired result, but when over or under used it becomes a demonstration of a different purpose. In the right proportion it can aid in meeting a production goal, but when used in excess in pursuit of a goal, the purpose now becomes to demonstrate power and not to achieve a goal. That makes for a temporary feel-good but damages trust and respect.

So many times, however, leaders make the mistake of finding fault with others for the purpose of revealing their weakness, and not to improve it, especially when the leader and the employee have an overlapping weakness.

Fail to treat others with respect, and respect will forever elude you. Give respect out freely and genuinely, and it will come back to you exponentially.

I (Janet) met with HR one day to discuss a VP of Sales who needed coaching. His employees would walk around the entire 90,000 square foot building in order to avoid walking down the hallway where the VP of Sales had his office, because they were afraid he would stop them in the hallway and demand information or chew them out for something. And they were deathly afraid to tell him when there was a mistake made.

The HR manager shared that this VP had already been talked to about his bullying behaviors and had previously had a coach, but now he was back to his old ways. I was called in with the hope that I could work with him from an inside-out development approach rather than a situational problem-solving approach.

After collecting the client's assessment results, I met with him for our first meeting. We had a terrific discussion, he embraced the process, and we were off to a good start. He asked if we could meet the following Friday at 9:00 a.m. rather than waiting two weeks. I checked my calendar and let him know that I already had an internal staff meeting but thought that I could change it and would get back to him.

On Wednesday morning the following week, I received a phone call from the client. He asked me in a very stern voice why I had not gotten back to him to confirm Friday. I felt so bad. He was right, I should have gotten back to him and I totally forgot.

With my tail between my legs, I completely apologized by letting him know how bad I felt and admitted that it was irresponsible of me to not have called earlier.

"Yes, I am still able to meet with you on Friday, unless you prefer to change it back to the originally scheduled time. That is okay with me as well," I said.

This time he responded, "You should have called me sooner! It is unacceptable for you to not follow up with me! You are supposed to be the example for leadership!"

I, again, apologized for my mistake.

Then he said, "I don't think that I can work with a coach who doesn't follow up when they say they will."

Again, for the third time, I genuinely apologized and promised him that I would never make that mistake again and that it was not my typical mode of operation. Then I asked him what he would like to do. He said that he would see me on Friday, and slammed the phone down.

At this point, I was beating myself up and knew that I had really messed up. I figured I might as well go to HR and let them know that they may need to find a new coach. Until it dawned on me. Perhaps his biggest challenge is forgiveness. Perhaps this is why people are afraid of him and why he berates people who make mistakes. My training *and background had me wondering if he had difficulty forgiving himself and that it is why he can't forgive others.*

So rather than make assumptions, I decided to approach him with this idea in our next coaching session. I decided to give him an experience that demonstrated vulnerability and let him know how it made me feel when he made me apologize three times instead of taking my first apology. I told him that, in that moment, I wanted to give up because I didn't know if I would ever get back in his good graces. I told him that forgetting to call him was a rare mistake for me to ever make and that because of his response, if I worked with him or for him, I may have decided to avoid him from then on.

I asked him if there was a possibility that this was happening in the workplace. It was a home run. He cried. He couldn't understand why he did that to people. We identified where his aggression came from, how to recognize the specific triggers that caused this behavior, what to do to replace the negative behavior with a positive behavior, and gave him a tool to start tracking his behaviors.

Over a relatively short period of time and after talking with his direct reports about his desire to improve, this VP of Sales started to gain trust and respect from his people instead of fear and avoidance. I had given him an experience to recognize his negative behavior, he really wanted to change, and he had a qualified coach to help support him in the process.

It is a common scenario for leaders to find themselves frustrated with the lack of results they are getting from others, and resort to fear tactics. But fear and intimidation aren't respected long term nor can respect be mandated. Talking loud, taking charge, making demands, and knowing every answer every time may seem like fostering respect, but these behaviors are perceived by others as disrespectful. At some point over the years these deficient leaders discover that they have been less than successful at developing trust and respect and instead of getting real, facing their issues head on, and putting a plan in place to solve them, they instead adopt a persona of *false respect* as a replacement for actual respect. It's like fools' gold—it looks like gold, like respect, but it isn't. Eventually this persona becomes them, and they empower this false respect with great energy, but they never seem to quite achieve the level of respect that they are looking for.

FOUR TYPES OF FALSE RESPECT

False respect as a leader comes in a number of forms, none of which lead to actual respect. These forms commonly surface as:

1. ***Respect through ENTERTAINMENT.*** Have you ever noticed the leader who is sarcastic and always cracking jokes? He wants to be seen as the leader by being the funny person, always having a humorous comment to demonstrate his association and competence. Unfortunately this often leads to using another person as the springboard to ridicule, and disguises true leadership with the notion that somehow humor demonstrates expertise and superiority. This comes at the cost of other people, and true leadership isn't accomplished at another person's demise.

   Understand, humor has its place in the relationship equation and even to demonstrate vulnerability as a leader, but when humor and sarcasm are overdone and used as a substitute for solid foundational leadership, then the role becomes unacceptable.

2. ***Respect through FEAR.*** Arguably a common form of false leadership in business is fear, often accompanied by misery and bullying. Bullies keep people on edge, making others always react because the staff is afraid of what the bully might do. This sense of power may feel good to the leader but it is not leadership. It can appear that this method is working because the leader sees people worried and busy, but it doesn't earn him respect as a leader, and it is certainly not sustainable.

   a. We have been asked many times to coach bully bosses (or fear motivators). As a result, we have studied the characteristics and behaviors that these bully bosses have in common so we may help other leaders with these natural tendencies to become aware of them before it costs them a relationship or job. These traits (and we are suggesting that a true bully has all of these traits, not just one or two) include:

   b. They have low learning abilities (verbal and/or written). When someone is not (or thinks he is not) as smart as others, he has difficulty explaining himself in a conversation and as such, he uses more forceful tones and language to stop others from asking questions or for more explanation.

c. They are competitive and have an extreme desire to win at the cost of others. If someone's desire to win exceeds their desire for the care and concern of others, then the leader won't care how something makes you feel, as long as the goal is met. So if the goal is met by using bully tactics they will continue to use them even at someone else's expense.

d. They have such a high need to be right and in charge, that being in charge negatively is better than not being in charge at all. If a boss believes that her beliefs and ways of doing things are always the best, she will insist on leading a team or project and devalue others' ideas, even if that action makes others mad, angry, or frustrated.

e. They process information through a feelings filter rather than a facts filter. Bully bosses have a tendency to react to whatever is said or done because they take many things personally. When someone is hard on himself, he ends up being hard on others.

f. They don't easily forgive other people's mistakes because they have difficulty forgiving themselves. If a bully was raised by a bully, or by someone who had difficulty accepting others as they are, then he may have a continuous conversation loop going on in his head that is reminding him he is a failure and not good enough.

Bully bosses use fear as a somewhat effective temporary motivator, forcing staff to double check, think thoroughly, and consider consequences, but the domination of fear is stifling and refocuses people to a task at the cost of losing identity with the overall purpose. Fear can have value as a short-term warning, like a performance improvement plan does in the workplace, but not as a substitute for respect.

3. **Respect by being a *KNOW-IT-ALL*.** Theoretically, the more you know, the more respect you are worthy of, right? Why then do people avoid know-it-alls? There is a common perception about a know-it-all that is visible to others but not

to the know-it-all himself. The suspicion is that the know-it-all's life has been absent of something in his past, and he is compensating for it by having to always demonstrate real-time knowledge of anything and everything. Unfortunately, this pretense of vast knowledge does not garner respect. It generates quite the opposite effect.

We were brought in by Human Resources to deliver a presentation to the executive team of a ski resort in hopes the CEO would see value in developing the team with our training. The presentation was about the ten mistakes teams commonly make.

About eight minutes into a one-hour presentation, the CEO interrupts in a rather matter-of-fact tone, announces that he doesn't believe his team needs development. He claims everyone trusts one another on his team and that his team works great together.

Rather than accept the premise of what he was saying, we challenged the team of ten people by asking if they agreed with his statement. Does everyone trust one another and is team development not necessary? The room was silent. No one spoke for about sixty seconds. Finally, one brave manager spoke up, expressing that he thought trust among team members could improve.

The CEO argued the point with the manager, defending his original judgment and shutting down all communication. Since he is the expert recruited from another successful ski resort, the CEO thinks he is the only one who knows what is best for the resort.

The CEO then turned to us, thanked us for coming and apologized for wasting our time. The HR manager was so embarrassed. As she walked us out she told us she was looking for a different job because the CEO thinks he knows what is best for his people, and he doesn't. She mentioned that employees don't trust him and, in fact, don't trust a few others on the executive team as well. Consequently communication was minimal and no one was willing to speak up, as evidenced in our meeting.

Know-it-alls aggravate other people because their conversations generally focus on themselves or attempt to prove their knowledge superiority. This mindset derails respect even if the information conveyed is accurate.

4. ***Respect through CONTROL.*** The controlling leader (sometimes viewed as a micro-manager) believes the more he controls, the greater his contribution and the more worthy he is of respect. However, that is not what happens. Occasionally, demonstrating control is quite necessary at the appropriate time to achieve the right outcome, but when used as a replacement for respect, control can demoralize an entire team and send individual worth into a spiral. It sends with it a message that "you cannot achieve my level of understanding." This does not lead to even the outer boundaries of developing respect. The process of controlling is often performed at the expense of another person's opinion and contribution. People who view control as competent leadership tend to ignore other leadership styles. Regretfully, they rarely explore an entire world of leadership through motivation and fostering critical thinking behaviors. The leader who has thankfully shed this form of false respect and moved into a realm of solid effective leadership may view this control-minded leader as stuck, unaware, and lacking in the ability to develop trust.

It can be observed that leaders who lead by these elements of false respect are focused on how they lead and have become detached with *why* they are the leader. They have disconnected with their purpose. After all, a leader who is in touch with the noble cause of developing other people and inspiring a motivational team environment can't possibly consider being a bully or a clown to achieve it.

STRATEGIES FOR BUILDING TRUST AND RESPECT

An effective leader must be able to interact with employees, peers, bosses and many other individuals both inside and outside the organization. In truth, leaders need to gain trust and respect in order to meet or exceed established objectives. Accomplish that and your success is imminent. Here are fourteen strategies that can bring this about:

1. **Make promises only when you are sure you can keep them.** Take making promises seriously. Don't make promises based only on good intentions of wanting to be reliable in the moment. Make promises you are reasonably sure you can execute. View a promise as a commitment made with an understanding that circumstances might arise that would make it impossible to keep. Make those circumstances very clear to the person at the time promises are made. Breaking a promise can lead to a loss of respect on the part of another. They may question or not trust your integrity or judgment. In that rare circumstance when you do break a promise, face the person eye-to-eye and explain in detail why you were not able to keep your promise. Be honest about it.

2. **Admit mistakes.** If others believe you are not aware of your mistakes, they are concerned you may make the mistakes again. When you admit a mistake, however, others can move on with the knowledge that you have the ability to self-correct.

Guidelines for giving a sincere apology:

1. Give a detailed account of the situation.
2. Acknowledge the hurt or damage done.
3. Recognize your role in the situation and take full responsibility.
4. Include a statement of regret.
5. Ask for forgiveness.
6. Say: "Here is what I am going to do."
7. Provide a form of restitution, if possible.

3. **Offer and accept apologies without hesitation.** Apologies have the power to heal humiliations, free the mind from guilt, remove the desire for vengeance, and ultimately restore relationships. When you accept an apology, avoid adding any judgment to it. For example, don't say, "That's fine, but I doubt that you're going to change," or "I'm sorry I embarrassed you in the meeting, but you see why I had to do it, don't you?" This type of response breeds resentment and there is *no* room for relationship building when one party holds bitterness for the other.

4. **Listen to others' complaints and problems.** No person thinks his troubles are insignificant. If you take another person's complaint lightly or ignore it altogether, a problem still exists. In fact it may grow and fester. An effective leader will address the grievance by listening and considering the potential seriousness of the situation. If the issue is trivial and the person is merely whining, a good leader isn't afraid to tell the person that and explain why, without any belittling. Even though the person may not hear the answer he is looking for, the leader will not lose respect due to inattention.

> **If someone comes to you with a complaint or a problem, your response after listening fully may sound like: "I hear your point of view and can see why you have come to this conclusion. Is there another way of looking at this situation that would be more productive?"**

5. **Show consistency and fairness in the treatment of others.** Do you vary your approach with others, being lenient with some and strict with others? Do you give more attention to some than others? There is a fine line between treating others exactly the same (applying identical methods to every individual) and showing consistency in the treatment of others (being kind to everyone equally but varying how you display your kindness). People are all individuals with different backgrounds, values, goals, ideas and motivational needs. You can treat people fairly yet differently. The ability to recognize the differences in people and the ability to apply variable leadership methodologies is an important characteristic of effective leadership.

6. **Keep sensitive information confidential.** In any relationship, personal or professional, confidentiality is imperative to building and maintaining trust. Decide at the end of conversations and meetings what information or decisions you will decide to share—with whom, and when. If someone shares with you something confidential, and you know that it could impact another negatively, encourage the person who

is sharing the news with you to go directly to the individual who may suffer from the impact.

7. **Talk Straight**. Trusted leaders are straight shooters who say what they mean and mean what they say, without letting potential conflict dilute the message. They don't confuse or mislead others by hinting, avoiding, or beating around the bush when they have a point to make. On the flipside, they also avoid judgment and aggressive language that is accusing or attacking but not descriptive. (See Exercise #3 at the end of this chapter.)

8. **Nurture positive self-esteem in others.** This key principle is essential to gaining trust in any environment. Positive, affirming behaviors go a long way toward establishing effective interactions. Remind others that they are valuable to you or to the company they work for. Notice people doing things right and use the opportunity for recognition. Point out specifics and tell them what you like about them. It makes your feedback more sincere.

> **Standing up for others may sound like: "I don't think that it is fair that you should be responsible for delivering this message by yourself to the executive team. Why don't we create some objective evidence to share with the team and then I will come with you to the meeting to add support and additional information."**

9. Stand up for others. For a company, team, or any community for that matter, to be successful, each member must be able to come to an important realization: "I am not alone." This can only happen in an environment of mutual trust and respect. To display this, when friends or coworkers find themselves in a difficult situation, share the responsibility for improving it. Colleagues need to know that you will focus on solving the problem, not on placing blame. In this way, you convey you are on the same side, and trust grows.

10. **Avoid gossip or unfair criticism of others**. Lies, exaggeration, gossip, and criticism all destroy an atmosphere of trust. Remember that because there are always problems, there are always opportunities to criticize someone else. When

this happens, of course, trust and respect erode. You can be a positive leader by working hard to provide balanced feedback, both on what others do well and what they can improve on, without joining in the gossip and the negative effects of criticism.

11. **Develop goals and objectives with others**. Any team of people--whether it is a marriage team, sports team, departmental team, or volunteer group of people who develop and agree upon goals together—succeeds when its members understand what is important. We have seen teams who are not in alignment or are not clear about their goals, resulting in members who "politic and position" their personal desires and agendas, which leads to mistrust among team members and ultimately mediocre results. In contrast, when members know that all other team members understand and agree to pursue the goals, they can trust their teammates to perform for the good of the team.

12. **Accept confrontation**. Fighting is not good, but neither is false agreement. If you find that others are reluctant to disagree with you, they may be afraid of confronting you. This occurs when there is confusion or when others fear you may be defensive. They will agree with you publicly without sharing their real thoughts, limiting success for everyone involved. Let others know you want to hear what they have to say, and when there is a difference of opinion, promote discussion. And remember… clarity is always more important than being right.

13. **Say "No" without creating resentment.** The ability to say no to others without creating hostility or resentment is important. The key is to recognize the request with sincerity and explain in detail why the request cannot be granted. You might say: "I really appreciate the fact that you would come to me for help, but right now, I have three other projects that are due tomorrow. Is this something that we could tackle at the end of the week?" Being sincere demonstrates concern and makes your personal regret believable.

14. **Deliver Results.** Nothing speaks louder than action. We have a tendency to judge ourselves based on our intent ("I

meant to be on time for the meeting"), but we judge others based on their actions ("He's late again"). Take an objective step back from your job and your relationships and assess the actual results you're delivering. Would others say they can rely on you to follow through on your projects and commitments?

TRANSPARENCY AND VULNERABILITY

Probably the most important trait that garners trust and respect is demonstrating a willingness to be transparent and vulnerable. This involves an improved understanding of ourselves. We need to humbly recognize and explore our strengths and weaknesses, our desires and goals to better the future, and gain the ability to become transparent about them. To consider transparency, think of a star pitcher who enters the locker room moments before the big game with his pitching arm wrapped in a bandage from wrist to shoulder. With no explanation, he begins to dress for the game while his team-mates stare at his wrapped injury with mixed horror and curiosity. How badly is he hurt? Will he be able to pitch? What is he hiding under that massive ace wrap? Unless the fellow player is willing to be vulnerable and reveal to his buddies the embarrassing truth that his little sister tattooed his arm with her favorite pink nail polish for good luck, fear and distrust will tarnish the game for everyone.

This metaphor applies to what you allow others to see of what is inside. Consider the diminished level of trust when someone discovers that you are actively concealing certain information or even simply not revealing it. Being transparent is when you reveal something that is important to you and perhaps embarrassing, or that makes you vulnerable. We call this *active revealing*, and it has great benefits.

We were conducting team training with a company and in our first exercise to build trust we presented the following five questions:

1. *Where did you grow up?*
2. *What is your birth order?*
3. *What was your biggest challenge growing up?*
4. *What is your biggest pet peeve?*
5. *What is a hobby or interest that you have?*

The key trust-building question to test for a group's transparency with each other is question #3 – biggest challenge growing up. Everyone has had a challenge of some kind during childhood, whether getting picked on for being the smallest or the tallest, or never getting asked out on a date, or having parents that divorced, etc. These experiences provide a common bond of sorts.

So in this particular group of executives, we listened as each individual shared their answers to these five questions, and when we got to one of the executives, he shared, "My biggest challenge growing up is that my mom and dad didn't get along." And then he quickly moved to answer the next question. He demonstrated that he wasn't willing to be transparent.

Interestingly, what came out later in that meeting was that the team didn't trust him. They said that they didn't know him. They felt that he kept critical pieces of information about what was going on in the field to himself.

The two-day team training was highly successful and this executive team adopted a new perspective on expectations and behaviors. So they decided to extend the same training with the next level of managers, and asked to participate in the training again.

This time, when we rolled out the five questions exercise, the previous executive who had answered with "his mom and dad didn't get along" and who had recognized his need for more transparency to garner trust in the previous training, responded this time with, "I witnessed my mother shoot and kill my father." Wow! This brings "not getting along" to a whole new level. The point is this, the executive realized and learned that to improve communication and accountability, he needed to become more transparent in his communication, and the motives he initially internalized for not being transparent had consequences and inhibited the development of a well-functioning team.

If you are willing to share your honest thoughts with others, they are more likely to believe in your willingness to speak the truth even when it is uncomfortable. Others feel like they can trust your intentions better because of your sincerity. Your communication becomes engaging, not guarded. Real issues get discussed, so there is less "talking behind someone's back." When people don't trust each other, the tough conversations don't happen, and that leaves everyone uneasy.

When you think of vulnerability, you might think of uncertainty, risk, and exposure. You may be concerned that if you share your real feelings or motives, or if you appear to not know something or expose your naïveté, someone might take negative advantage of your vulnerability and use it against you. You may be afraid of rejection or being judged. But the truth is that most often your openness unlocks the door for others to share their own vulnerabilities.

> *At a new CEO roundtable group, we asked everyone to introduce themselves. Like typical CEOs, there was a little bit of "chest puffing" in their introductions. As we got just a little over halfway around the room, it was Lisa's turn. Lisa is a successful CEO of a medium-sized engineering firm. She spoke timidly. "Gosh, I don't have near the accomplishments any of you have. In fact, I don't think I am a very good CEO... I can't even read financial statements. So hopefully I can learn something from everyone else here."*
>
> *The room was silent. Her vulnerability and transparency changed the introduction approach of the remaining CEOs. There was less "chest puffing" and more transparency, and the other CEOs whom she had been a bit intimidated to follow, became a bit intimidated to follow her because she got real, and eliminated the time and place for bragging. It just didn't fit anymore. Lisa's transparency led to open, honest communication.*
>
> *As a result, this table of CEOs started discussing real issues quicker than most groups. They opened up to reveal their struggles and quickly learned they could trust each other because they all shared similar issues. We observed how the other CEOs started asking Lisa questions and wanted feedback from her. If we were to pick one CEO we all learned the most from in that CEO roundtable group, it was Lisa, and the lesson learned was how trust and respect can be achieved in an atmosphere of transparency.*

As a team leader, you can pave the way to help others enter safely into transparency by demonstrating openness and listening with respect. When a team or group of people, whether a sports team, departmental team, or family, become transparent with one another, they can move forward, trusting in the agreed upon responsibilities and expectations.

Understand that the primary motive for not being transparent is the worry of being judged, and there is a fasttrack solution to moving past this stifling hang-up. The quickest way to adopting a mindset of not worrying about being judged is for you to quit judging other people or criticizing them for their weaknesses. Those who worry the most about being judged are often the biggest violators of doing the judging. When you judge other people you keep judgment on the radar as a filter through which all is perceived. When the judgment radar is constantly on for another, you keep it constantly on for yourself as well. The beauty is, you have control over turning it off. Quit judging other people, and watch your own transparency become more natural.

Transparency will only build trust when it is not motivated by personal gain. The leader who competently manages the desire to contribute to the greater good is already building trust. When a worthy outcome is in mind, and transparency is evident in your communication, not only will people listen to you, they will trust and respect you.

ADVICE FROM YOUR COACH

Make a 30 day chart of the 14 Trust and Respect building strategies from this chapter and checkmark the amount of times that you violated trust and respect or garnered trust and respect.

LEADERSHIP EXERCISES
TRUST AND RESPECT

Leadership Exercise #3: TALK STRAIGHT

Exercise Purpose: To become a more trusted leader by effectively establishing direct communication habits.

The following exercise will allow you to clarify the differences between indirect communications (neither clear nor straightforward) and direct communications (both clear and straightforward).

Scenario: Have you ever encountered an office *schmoozer*? That is a person who visits you frequently during work hours with a strong need for conversation about non-work-related matters, such as office gossip, sports, or the latest movies, and who infringes on your privacy and robs you of time to get your work done. Sometimes you get rid of the schmoozer with some excuse, but he or she doesn't pick up on your hints. You realize that the time has come to address the problem. How might you deal with this situation? Thinking of your approach, write in the space below exactly what you would say to them.

_____
_____
_____
_____
_____
_____
_____
_____

Is your approach both clear and straightforward or is it excessively wordy so as to avoid conflict? How do you know? Does it address the problems the person is causing or are you just sharing your opinion? Do you offer a solution or just describe the problem? Look at the example below, would you say that your approach looks more like the direct scenario or the indirect scenario? Now think of someone who is direct in his/her communication whom you respect. Ask this person how he/she would handle the above scenario.

EXAMPLE:

DIRECT	INDIRECT
"Our conversations about non-work related things have been fun, but I have noticed in the last month, that we have spent an average of two hours a week in social conversation. I have many projects on my plate that need my focused attention. Would you mind if we keep our social conversations to lunch time or after work hours from now on?"	"Hey, I have so much work to get done that I am overwhelmed. You know my boss is demanding more and more from me and it's becoming difficult to manage. Maybe we should meet for lunch more often so that we have time to socialize. I think if I could just focus on this one project over the next couple of weeks without interruptions that it will get better. So, I really need to get back to work. Are you available for lunch?"

Additional practice scenarios to determine whether you are direct or indirect.

How would you handle:

- Someone who has taken credit for something you have done.
- Someone who has not kept a promise, resulting in a very undesirable consequence.
- Someone who continually disagrees with you.
- Someone who keeps bad-mouthing another person.
- Someone who has not followed through on a commitment he/she made to you.
- An employee who reports to you who is continually late for work.

Leadership Exercise #4: TRUST QUESTIONNAIRE

Exercise Purpose: To gauge the level of trust others have in you. On the following page is a self-assessment to help you identify whether you are building trust with others or possibly tearing it down. The intent is to gather perceptions on whether you are a trustworthy person deserving of respect. Consider going to our website: www.TheEmployersEdge.com to download copies of this questionnaire and give it to at least three people who know you best, not necessarily the people who like you the most. Give it to a family member, a close friend, and someone you work with. Then match their answers against your answers. Identify the areas that need the most improvement and go to work on them.

Expected Outcome: To have identified the behaviors that may be causing others to distrust you. Once identified, you can use the strategies mentioned in this chapter to regain trust with people whose trust you have broken, as well as take action to behave in a way that is consistent with the trusting person you would like to become.

For a FREE download of this questionnaire (in a version for other people to rate you), go to TheEmployersEdge.com.

TRUST QUESTIONNAIRE

In an effort to develop trust and respect with others, respond to each statement as accurately as possible by circling the number that best expresses the degree to which you believe the statement describes me or is true of me. Circle a "5" if you would say the statement "always" describes my actions or a "1" if the statement "never" describes my actions.

QUESTION	No or Never			Yes or Always
1. I am able to admit if I have done something wrong.	1 2	3	4 5	
2. I demonstrate transparency by sharing appropriate personal information about myself.	1 2	3	4 5	
3. I avoid embarrassing or making fun of others.	1 2	3	4 5	
4. I treat others equally, looking beyond stereotypes and prejudices, and embrace others' uniqueness.	1 2	3	4 5	

QUESTION	No or Never		Yes or Always
5. I say "please" and "thank you" and show tangible ways of honoring others.	1 2	3	4 5
6. I give my full attention when you or someone else is talking.	1 2	3	4 5
7. I respect and honor the policies and procedures of the organization that I work for.	1 2	3	4 5
8. I value others' feelings, property, and belongings.	1 2	3	4 5
9. You and others come to me for personal and/or professional advice.	1 2	3	4 5
10. I keep my promises.	1 2	3	4 5
11. I speak well of others and never say unkind things behind their backs.	1 2	3	4 5
12. I avoid holding onto anger and sincerely accept others' apologies.	1 2	3	4 5
13. I effectively apologize to others when I have done them wrong.	1 2	3	4 5
14. I am open to differing points of view and genuinely take others' ideas into consideration.	1 2	3	4 5
15. I say "no" when I mean no and "yes" when I mean yes.	1 2	3	4 5
16. I show consistency and fairness in the treatment of others.	1 2	3	4 5
17. I communicate without belittling or sounding condescending.	1 2	3	4 5
18. I demonstrate competence in my work.	1 2	3	4 5
19. I ask people questions about their personal opinions and life experiences.	1 2	3	4 5
20. I avoid "going around others" to get my needs met.	1 2	3	4 5
21. Others openly discuss their problems and concerns with me.	1 2	3	4 5
22. I meet deadlines and follow through on my commitments.	1 2	3	4 5
23. I will defend another person if someone is speaking to them or treating them unfairly.	1 2	3	4 5
24. I avoid sharing confidential information with others.	1 2	3	4 5
25. I avoid language that shames others. Such as "You're not going to (wear that/say that/do that) are you?"	1 2	3	4 5
26. People do not have to walk on pins and needles around me.	1 2	3	4 5

Beyond Words

The impression that they have of you
Is not what you convey.
You've never said a single word
To make them think that way.

Yet still somehow they would conclude
You are who you are not,
So what you do to change it
Is beyond your very thought.

Consider this and realize
Come next time you choose,
You say things in so many ways
Beyond the words you use.

You say it in the way you dress,
You say it in your gait,
You say it every time you guess
Instead of shooting straight.

You say it in your tone of voice,
You say it with your eyes,
You say it when you make a choice
And when you compromise.

You say it when you look within,
You say it when you're late,
You say it every time you sin
And when you vacillate.

You say it when you disrespect,
You say it in dismay,
You say it when your actions
Fall short of what you say.

By Ed Beard, Copyright 2015

Competency Three
INTEGRITY

In this Chapter, we will:

- Define reference points and learn to identify and live from your values as a key personal development strategy.

- Show you how to respect people who don't align with your values system.

- Demonstrate how to identify your leadership values and communicate them to the people you are responsible for developing.

- Give you an exercise to help you determine your personal life values and how to live according to what is most important to you.

Chapter Three
INTEGRITY

You know leaders have integrity when their behaviors are consistent with their values, even when it is inconvenient.

People with integrity are characterized as individuals who can be counted on to do what is consistently right. They are reliable and predictable in dealing with others and with issues. They are defenders of what is fair, just, and acceptable. Leaders with integrity will do what they say even in the midst of an easier less conflicting option. Their words and deeds match up. They won't twist facts for personal advantage. They are careful to keep promises, and they can be counted on to tell the truth.

Integrity starts with knowing and acting upon your values and recognizing your boundaries. Leaders with integrity make better decisions because they have a *reference point* with which to measure a decision.

The San Joaquin Valley in California is known for its rich agriculture. It is flat, hot, and many of the towns are small and supported by farming. The Valley is also known for its tremendously dense fog; fog so incredibly thick that both ends of Walmart are not visible at the same time, and it can set in in a matter of minutes.

One morning while driving from Fresno to Lemoore, the fog set in so thick that the road itself became hard to see. Being surrounded by something that you can't reach out and touch makes for an eerie feeling, but I (Ed) had made this drive so many times I was in no worry of getting lost. I invariably ended up getting stuck behind a slow and cautious driver who was having a difficult time making her way. As my patience got tested, I pulled up on her rear end, then backed off, then pulled up close, then backed off. After a while, it got so frustrating that I decided passing was a better option, so I pulled out into the oncoming lane and started to pass her. As I moved up alongside, the car that was in front was now out of sight, leaving me to cut the fog, and that took on a whole different feel. Instinctively I backed off the gas because I realized I was going too fast and the best thing to do was to slow down and pull back in behind the car that had been in front of me. You see, that car was a reference point for me and gave me a sense of location, speed and distance. Without it, those senses were gone.

If you've ever driven in such dense fog, you have most likely experienced times when the car starts to shake and shudder, and you realize you have drifted across the oncoming lane or onto the shoulder. With such extremely limited vision, it is normal to run through stop signs and past gas stations without even seeing them. I remember one time approaching the red light at an intersection only to get close and discover the red light was actually a running light on the back of a semi-trailer.

When you are traveling along a familiar drive, such as I was this particularly foggy day, you are in danger of being led by a false sense of confidence, and think you are somewhere that you are not. After all, you reason, you've driven this commute so many times you could drive it in your sleep. But when you are unable to see the familiar reference points, you may instead end up in a town miles away from your destination.

Later in the day when the fog lifts and the newscaster reports all of the accidents on the California highway, some of the accidents may have involved sixty cars and happened over a period of two hours. From the helicopter view, you might notice five cars or more neatly lined up behind each other all sitting in a ditch. The lead car, the reference point, had driven into the ditch and the cars behind it naturally followed one by one. As they played follow the leader none of these drivers knew they were drifting off the road until it was too late.

Drivers often don't even realize the reference points they use to get from one place to another, but they are there, know it or not. The dead tree before an intersection is just an absent glance, but for years it has told a driver's subconscious that the intersection is approaching so be ready. In the fog, that reference point is as good as gone and so is any thought of an approaching intersection.

Sometimes maneuvering in the fog can be so confusing that a natural inclination is to pull to a stop on the foggy road because you can't see what's ahead of you. This is exceptionally dangerous because another vehicle is sure to smash into your parked car from behind; and worse case scenario… it could be a semi-tractor trailer hauling fertilizer. Business can take on that same feel.

It's foggy out there on the business road and knowing who to follow or which direction to steer is difficult. Sometimes the best thing to do is to stop and regain your bearings, but if you stop for too long the world can rear-end you, causing a massive accident. If you don't pay careful attention, your over-confidence can mislead you in the wrong direction. And if you follow another leader blindly you may end up in the ditch, far from your goals and in places you hadn't intended to go.

This points out the importance of carefully choosing your reference points.

When you think about it, there is actually a reliable reference point for drivers that will get your vehicle to your destination in the fog every time. It is always there and notifies you when approaching an intersection, when to turn, and when to stop. It keeps you out of the ditch or from drifting into oncoming traffic, and because it is there it provides assurance to keep moving ahead, thus avoiding that feeling of helplessness and the need to stop.

That reference point is the little white line in the middle of the road.

Get too close to it and danger is at hand from oncoming traffic. Get too far away and the ditch on the right side is eminent. That little white line will always be in the middle of the road and it will keep you safe and in the lane, but only if you know to keep your eyes on it as your reference point.

Good reference points, whether on the drive or in business, are stable and dependable, remaining consistent over time. You can trust in their integrity. Bad reference points shift and vary. When people follow reference points that change, they can head down the wrong road completely unaware, convinced they're on the right road. But when we set our sights on solid, reliable reference points, they will stop us from going on unintended journeys that take us miles from our destination, and stop us from kidding ourselves into thinking we know right where we are. Good reference points give us a framework that allows us to keep moving so life doesn't smash us from behind. The scope of our achievements, the size of our thoughts, our happiness and graciousness, are all determined by not only what we choose to use as our reference point, but also by our commitment to adhere to it.

Your values keep you out of the ditch, they let other people know that you won't lead them into the ditch, and they alarm you when danger is approaching. Personal values help determine priorities, a way of life, as well as social, political, religious, and business interactions. Consider your values as your white line, your reference point, that keeps you on the road and moving forward.

What is your reference point? How do you know it's a good one? What is that *one* thing that you can keep your eye on that never changes, that you can see, and that will guide you to where you want to go every time, especially when the road ahead isn't so clear?

Just as the white line in the middle of the road guides your commute, your *values* serve as your life-guiding and decision making reference point.

Each of us holds many values and these values are liable to develop as we grow, reach different stages of life or have different experiences and influences in life. Our values evolve from a range of sources. Parents play a key influence upon our values as we grow as children. So, too, does any "higher being," church, or religious background we experience. Our society, our neighbors, friends and colleagues can have an influence upon our values, as can our teachers and our schooling. As we grow in years and experience, our values become more fixed. We call these long-term and time-tested values our *core values*.

Core values determine what is most important to us as an individual, as a leader, or in defining corporate culture. They are shaped by our past, and can be cultivated for our future. As we mature and develop, we gain the ability to choose values that are most currently vital to us. Common leadership core values may be: honesty, courage, timeliness, initiative, dependability, strategic and critical thinking, among many others. (You will be given the opportunity to explore more core values in the exercises at the end of this chapter.) It is important to know your core values and to be able to define the behaviors that demonstrate those values so that you make choices that line up with your goals.

In the fall of 2015, the National Football Foundation announced the induction of one of the most successful college football coaches in the nation. Bill Snyder is known for his long-term accomplishments at Kansas State, most noteably for perhaps the greatest turnaround in the history of college football.

When Coach Snyder arrived at K-State, the football team was in the midst of a 0-26 losing streak and had only been in a bowl game once in its first ninety-three seasons. Under his leadership over the next twenty-three years, his young athletes went on to win nearly eighty percent of their games, clinching multiple titles championships including Big 12 Championship and National Number One rankings.

Besides being known for his outstanding coaching success, Bill Snyder is perhaps most famous for his *16 Goals for Success*. Coach holds steadfastly to this list of core values and leads his teams consistently with them. He insists that when the K-State Wildcats have seen their greatest success is when the highest percentage of players adopt the *16 Goals* as well. As he teaches the goals to his athletes, he explains, "These are lessons of life that will help you on the field, but also off the field in life."

Coach Bill Snyder's *16 Goals for Success* are:

1. Commitment
2. Unselfishness
3. Unity
4. Improve
5. Be Tough
6. Self-Discipline
7. Great Effort
8. Enthusiasm
9. Eliminate Mistakes
10. Never Give Up
11. Don't Accept Losing
12. No Self-Limitations
13. Expect to Win
14. Consistency
15. Leadership
16. Responsibility

Often questioned about his list, Bill Snyder says, "They come from my mother (Marionetta). The foundation comes from how she raised me, and what she meant to me. How you buy into those values is who you are."

When you act consistently with your core values, you are living with integrity. Integrity here doesn't mean honesty or honor—it means *being true to yourself.*

At the apex of life, the "you" at work and the "you" at home are the same "you." We hear much too frequently "I am a very different person at home than I am at work." Then where do you not get to be the real "you"? Home or work? Do you fake one or the other and is there authenticity that garners respect and leadership if you're not being your natural self? To be a good leader you need to be congruent. You need to be aware of your core values and embrace the freedom for you to be *you* at all times. That is integrity.

Think of the freedom that comes with a commitment to this level of personal integrity. If I seek to be true to myself, knowing my strengths and weaknesses, and accept myself for these, I become a more empathetic person. I begin to understand others better and look at their situations from their viewpoint, not my own. I don't have to fake interest, understanding, care or concern. I can genuinely love others, because I can love myself. Why can I love myself? Because I am not putting forth an image that is not real or fraudulent.

Many people are uncomfortable with this idea because they may not think that the "real me" is a good enough person. But in this book, you will see that the "real you" is better than the role you think you have to play at work. With the proper awareness and a few leadership exercises, we hope you will discover that the "real you" fits well in both places without the artificial persona in one of them.

Living a life of integrity means putting actions behind your words, like developing a key personal development strategy of learning to identify and live from your values.

The surprising thing is that if you ask most people what their values are, many would not be able to give you an answer. Many people are leading lives oblivious of their core values. This can lead to a life of unhappiness, discontent and lack of fulfillment. People who don't know their values tend to wander, bouncing from one job or activity to another, trying to find themselves, forever ungrounded.

They're like puppets, pulled along without any clear direction.

Knowing your core values helps you:

- Follow a clear set of rules and guidelines for your actions. You're less likely to take the easy way out or chase after short-term gains at the expense of your long-term goals.
- Make good decisions. You quickly know what good choices are for you and what are not. For example, let's say you are leading a team of people and you have "customer first" in your mission statement or values list. Then someone on the team suggests that you discontinue a product or service that your customers have shared give them the greatest value over any other product or service that you offer. You will be able to quickly decide that discontinuing this product (while least profitable for you) does not meet the number one value of your team or organization... Customers first!
- Find compatible people, places, jobs, and activities that support your way of living. Imagine looking for a spouse or new job, but not really knowing what is important to you. What happens is one of two things – either everything is important therefore never reaching a decision to marry or accept a job, or nothing is clear thereby landing you multiple spouses and jobs until you find the best one that "feels" right at the time.

To be a leader who has integrity, you need to identify your values and demonstrate consistency in them. Elements of leadership change with the times, with the world and with the business, but when leaders change their *core values*, they are no longer a good reference point for other people. For example, if the customer truly comes first, and another employee hears you unfairly bad mouthing a customer, you're not living with integrity and you are now a variable reference point, making your leadership unreliable.

Leaders without a solid reference point, without honorable core values, without integrity, have a way of drifting into the ditch without knowing it until it's too late, with their team following right behind them.

One time in a Train The Internal Coach® event, we were again teaching leaders how to execute on the values exercise. The leader who volunteered had a list of six or seven values that she shared with the group and on that list was the value of discipline. She described discipline as doing the same thing the same way every time at the same time. When asked why this is a value, she responded 'discipline keeps people focused, on task, and away from distractions which results in better performance. Discipline also makes a leader predictable because their team knows what to expect.' She then went on to share that 'another critical value was flexibility. If something isn't getting a result then do it differently. Don't get so stuck in your ways that you don't consider better methods. People have to change as business requires change.' As you can see, this opened up a meaty discussion. She herself had conflicting values and she didn't even realize it. Do things the same way every time but do things differently when you need to. Her people had no idea when to be disciplined and when to be flexible, and neither did she.

It is important for you as a leader to list your values, define them, and communicate them to your team. It may be difficult, but there is something to gain. Integrity is not going to just get handed to you. You will have to earn it. Every time a value gets tested, it is an opportunity to demonstrate integrity.

Two primary reasons that people don't want to communicate their values is that 1) they really don't want to commit to them, and 2) they don't want to be judged when they fall short of meeting their own values. But the truth is that a leader who won't share his full list of values in fear he might be caught violating one of them actually becomes the fog, creating confusion and uncertainty for everyone. A leader who wants the flexibility of living outside of her own values in case honoring a value becomes difficult in a given situation damages her integrity because a value only takes on meaning when it holds up under difficult scrutiny. What good is having a value of quality if the need for quality never comes into play or if reducing quality allows you to meet a deadline and retain the customer?

So how do you as a leader demonstrate integrity and live according to your values—your system of what is right and wrong—and how can you operate from a place of integrity with people who don't align with similar values? To become a leader of integrity, you must communicate your values and supporting behaviors to people, and then allow them to communicate the same in return. As you gain understanding of another person's values you demonstrate respect for that individual. To be clear, the goal is not to adopt another person's values, but to respect the fact they may be different from yours. Only in this way will others be able to develop respect for you, and only through good communication will they become aware of the virtues of your values and how they can benefit from them. Let people know what you value most and expect of them, so that you set them up to win with you. Show them how acting in accordance with your values benefits them as well.

Years ago, I (Janet) was on assignment with a Fortune 500 company, training the managers of the marketing department to lead their people more effectively. Because this training program included one-on-one coaching for all eleven managers, we got to know some of the leadership values instilled in the Vice President of Marketing. One of her core values was timeliness. She shared with us the difficulty she was having with one of her managers who was also attending the training class. This manager missed three out of every four deadlines and she was tired of it as it was making her look bad.

During a particular session, we were conducting one of our leadership modules that helps leaders understand the needs of their staff, what makes them tick, and how to manage accordingly. One of the exercises is simply called "The Leadership Values Exercise." After we took the team through the process of identifying their personal leadership values (their system of what is right and wrong in how they lead and manage themselves and others), we asked for two volunteers to share their list. The VP of Marketing volunteered her list of ten values and at the top was "timeliness and meeting deadlines." Then we asked the manager who was about to lose her job for her list. At the top of her list was "quality of work." For this VP and one of her managers, these two values were in conflict with each other, yet both were vital to their internal and external customer who demanded high quality and firm deadlines. The fact is, if the VP had fired her manager and hired someone who met every deadline, she may have lost out on the quality of product her department was able to produce.

When the training was over, I met first individually with both the VP and the manager in question. What I learned was that the manager, who wanted quality, felt that her boss wasn't educating her internal and external clients on the time needed to produce quality work. I evaluated her statement against her assessment scores, recognizing that in fact this manager was capable of a great volume of work, and that perhaps the VP wasn't educating or pushing back enough.

I then conducted a coaching session with the VP. Recognizing that she avoided conflict and wanted to please her internal customers, I coached her on how to have the conversations with her internal customers to set realistic deadlines and expectations.

Then I got the two leaders together and they agreed upon three new commitments: 1) The manager would provide a regularly updated list of projects so that the VP could better understand the volume of work taking place in the manager's department, 2) the VP, when possible, would not make any final time commitments without checking with her departmental manager, 3) the departmental manager would conduct a competency analysis on her direct reports to see if all team members were operating at full capacity.

So the training exercise of understanding team members' values ended up producing higher quality work, meeting deadlines, and avoided losing a valuable manager.

For some leaders a conflict can arise within them because they are trying to live a life according to the values of a company, a religious or political organization, even the values of their friends or colleagues, rather than living a life according to their own core values. In doing this, the values of the other people or organizations are being met but the person's own values are being left unfulfilled and sapping them of energy. This is not to say that a person is always wrong to support the values of other people or organizations. However, contradicting your own values can lead to frustration and unhappiness.

We have also seen circumstances in the course of business when the organization or a boss forces an employee to act against her values. Perhaps a sales representative is forced to lie to a customer about a quality control failure or the reason for a low order fill rate. Perhaps an executive leader observes a peer pass the blame on a critical component that was left out of a contract, which is now going to cost the company millions of dollars. These scenarios are common and very real, so how should they be addressed?

Recently we were engaged in a coaching venue with a Vice President of Operations and her team of approximately 140 people. She shared a circumstance she was currently facing that was forcing her to act in a manner that violated her personal value of fairness, and asked us for some perspective on it. The organization had just completed their annual reviews. Following protocol due to the results of the reviews, she took measures to terminate the bottom eleven poor performers, which then increased her average appraisal score significantly when compared to other departments. With the bottom eleven people now gone, she had too many people fall into the "exceptional" category as a percentage. This red-flagged at the executive level, and she was instructed to get her average performance appraisal scores back down so they were more in line with the other departments. She explained that the reason her average scores were so comparatively high was because she had eliminated the bottom eleven employees who were poor performers and who were costing the company more in salaries than they were producing. She defended her remaining team's average appraisal increase and attempted to avoid being penalized for showing good leadership and managing her people, but to no avail.

She wrestled with how she would go back to her team leaders and inform them that although they had worked hard, demonstrated commitment, and scored above the average, they were not going to be rewarded for the full value of their efforts. Their higher appraisal scores needed to be reduced to those of other departments, and their raises would reflect average appraisal scores and not exceptional appraisal scores that were legitimately earned.

This was a blatant violation of the VP's value of fairness, but she also had a value of accountability to the organization so without passing blame she followed through on the executive order. What further complicated the situation was that the organization had "treat each employee with respect" as a value, stated in the company mission statement and posted for all to see, and this directive was clearly in conflict with that value. As a result the company was suffering from damaged trust and respect.

It can be a difficult situation when achievement is not recognized as promised and a process seemingly has greater importance than a person. The way to unstick people past the obvious unfairness is to get them to think bigger. In this case I coached them to first disconnect the action from the attitude. Yes, I validated, they had good reason to feel treated unfairly, however they could choose to be positive despite the unfair environment. And I showed the VP how to demonstrate the common occurrence of inconsistency in an effort to help her team cut the company some slack.

So the VP gathered her team together and asked her people to write down what they want to be known for. She then had each member share their thoughts with the group. She heard statements like "I want to be known for treating people with respect, being positive, and being reliable and honest." To demonstrate the inconsistency in human nature, she then asked the team how dwelling on the unfair compensation plan earned them respect or cast them as being positive. They fought that for a bit with responses like "this is different," and "yeah but...." Ultimately, they had to admit that complaining about the source of their paycheck wasn't positive and they were not even honoring their own values. They then committed to demonstrating leadership by taking control of their attitudes and using a good attitude as the reference point for their teams.

With a frank and truthful tone, she also asked the group if acting in congruence with their values has ever imposed unfairness to another person, but to honor their values they had to do it. After everybody put their hands down, she reinforced that the company had to do what circumstances deemed right even if it landed on the team in a shadow of unfairness. If people give themselves the right to do this, then to be fair, they have to give the company the same right. Be consistent.

Although the sting was still noticeable as people left the meeting, they took control of their attitudes and went back to work because she got her people to think bigger by using herself as a bigger world reference point.

If you are the leader and your team is using you as their reference point, are you leading them with a fixed and reliable set of values that will lead them to success? We suggest that if a leader can answer yes to that question, he is a leader with integrity. The size and scope of your leadership effectiveness will be predicated on your integrity as a foundational reference point that can lead others through, and beyond, the fog.

The Difference between Values and Boundaries

Similar to values but not quite the same, are boundaries or guidelines. These boundaries are rules or limits that are created to identify for yourself what is reasonable, safe, and permissible ways for other people to behave around you and with you. Boundaries communicate to others the things that you *will* and *won't* tolerate, along with the outer limits of choices and freedoms people can engage in without offending you or involving you. Your boundaries are an extension of your values.

When you have not set your own boundaries, you leave them susceptible to getting tested for clarity by others. If not careful, this is when other people set your boundaries for you by virtue of the mere fact that your lack of a boundary is their license to do so.

A friend that I (Ed) would see from time to time was in sales and spent most of his time traveling in the western region of the United States to consult with clients. Every time I would see him, he would complain to me that the other sales reps didn't visit their clients as often as he did. He'd grumble that when he took the job, he had not signed up to travel five days a week. His boss was constantly nagging him to get in front of clients and close more sales, and he felt like an absent dad since he was unable to attend his children's school programs, help them with homework, or be there during the week for dinner and family time.

My friend valued his responsibility to the people he cared for, but he lacked the boundaries necessary to abide by that value. Therefore, other people had set unreasonable boundaries for him, causing him to feel anger and resentment.

When I asked him why he accepted his travel schedule, he shared that he was afraid his sales would slip, that he might get fired from his job, and that he couldn't support his family financially. His fear and self-doubt were overpowering his values and impeding his personal desires and goals. I coached him to set some definable boundaries such as "I will not travel more than three days per week." I explained that boundaries were necessary to live the quality of life he was wanting, and that since he wasn't setting his own boundaries, the universe along with the people in it were setting them for him. He didn't like the boundaries they were giving him that he now felt obliged to abide by.

"So give yourself the permission to set boundaries and work to preserve them," I urged.

Many people believe they should be able to cope with a situation or say yes because they're a good employee, manager, husband or wife, daughter or son, even though they may feel drained or taken advantage of. They may wonder if they even deserve to have boundaries in the first place. Many grew up in the role of caretaker, where they learned to focus on others, letting themselves be drained emotionally or physically. Ignoring their own needs may have become the norm.

Boundaries aren't just a sign of healthy relationships; they're a sign of self-respect. Setting boundaries keeps you in control of your time and efforts, which in return makes you feel better about yourself. This leads to a healthy self-image and greater effectiveness.

Good, decent people set boundaries. Boundaries are the way you take care of yourself. You have both a right and a duty to protect and defend yourself. When you establish boundaries that are based on your core values, others will recognize your integrity and respect you for it. Actually, establishing boundaries makes you a safe person, while not setting boundaries can foster a perception of doubt, weakness, incompatibility, and mystery. Let people know where they stand with you.

Consider these four different types of boundaries (that you will also find in Exercise #6 at the end of this chapter):

- **Material boundaries** – determine whether you give or lend things, such as your money, car, clothes, books, food, etc. If you have the value of helpfulness, you may establish the boundary that others can borrow items from you if they ask for permission first and agree to a reasonable return time.

- **Physical boundaries** pertain to your personal space, privacy, and body. How do you feel about loud music, and closed doors at work? Do you give a handshake or a hug – to whom and when is this appropriate? With a value of self-respect, your boundary may end at a handshake. If self-respect is not present, other people sense this and may test the boundary, and that could lead to a lingering touch or an inappropriate gesture.

- **Mental boundaries** apply to your thoughts, values, and opinions. Do you know what you believe, and will you defend your opinions? Can you listen with an open mind to someone else's opinion without becoming rigid? A healthy mental boundary drawn from the value of respect will prevent you from giving unwanted advice or getting into a senseless argument.

- **Emotional boundaries** separate the responsibility of your emotions from someone else's. They protect you from feeling guilty for someone else's negative feelings or problems and taking others' comments personally.

It is helpful to not only identify your personal boundaries, but your leadership boundaries. Go back through the list of the four boundaries and start determining what you will stand for – what is right and wrong – what you will and won't tolerate. Identify your material, physical, emotional, and mental limits. Consider what you can tolerate and accept and what makes you feel uncomfortable or stressed. Those feelings will help you identify what your limits are.

Write your boundaries down, and follow through on them. Ideally, **boundary setting needs to include 1) the behavior that is unacceptable, 2) the impact that it is having, and 3) a consequence if it continues. The following are some examples:**

- **Anger** – "Please stop yelling at me, it feels disrespectful. If you don't stop, I will leave the room."

- **Criticism**—"It's not okay for you to make comments about losing my hair. It is disrespectful and demeaning. If you don't stop I will leave the table and we won't be able to continue spending time together."

- **Time Pressure**—"I have a policy of not making snap decisions. I need time to think and reflect on what I want to do. If you need an immediate answer then it will be a NO."

- **Extra commitment**—"Although this looks like an important project, I need to decline your request for help because I have three other things that are a priority for me right now." (A consequence may need to be included in this example if this becomes a situation where someone is always delegating their work to you and they need to take personal responsibility instead.)

- **Money**—"I won't be lending you any more money. It is hard for me to plan around my budget when this happens. I care about you and your need to start taking responsibility for yourself."

When you do this for yourself, and those unforeseen circumstances arise, you will notice a little voice in your mind saying "alert, alert, warning, warning," and you'll know it's time to exercise your boundaries. Your boundaries will inspire you to take a stand, to say, "I am not going to do that, or this is not who I am." You may not be accepted in the moment, but you will be respected more in the long run.

Of course, when you stand firm in your boundary there is always the possibility that someone who doesn't want to be embarrassed will react in a way that embarrasses you first. But it will be temporary. When you enable others by giving in to their every whim, like a spoiled child or employee, you keep them from becoming conscious of their own behavior that is keeping them from experiencing growth through productive change.

Boundaries allow others to learn and grow.

Years ago, I (Janet) received very difficult feedback from my business partner Ed. He was setting a boundary with me. He told me that he was no longer willing to tolerate a growing behavior that he was seeing in me. He said that I often disrespected him in meetings, that I cut him off in communication, and that I didn't ask him enough questions to try to understand his viewpoint when he shared opinions and ideas. This explained why I would see him demonstrate frustration or walk out of a meeting. His boundary was very hurtful to hear, especially since I cared about Ed and our partnership. My first thinking was to defend myself. But I couldn't do the very thing he was accusing me of. In my desire to understand and grow, his boundary helped me to realize that I was at fault and that I was the one who needed to change. That in fact I was doing, in real time, the very behavior he accused me of. It hurt to think of others in my life and lifetime that I may have done that to as well. But thanks to Ed setting a boundary, I became the beneficiary of a behavior change that has helped me grow and improve.

Successful people set, and respect, boundaries. It is important to allow others to set their own boundaries without your input or judgment. If they are telling you what is acceptable or not acceptable for them, don't minimize their boundary with belittlement or laughter. Respect for others' boundaries will build on your relationship with that person. If they don't tell you what they are, ask them. With people who have similar personality types and values alignment, this creates little challenge. However, if you are boundary setting with someone who has a different communication style, personality or cultural background, boundary setting may need to be a little more direct. Also, consider the people you surround yourself with. Are the relationships reciprocal? Is there a healthy give and take? Exercise your integrity by examining your values and boundaries. Be a leader who is a worthy reference point.

ADVICE FROM YOUR COACH

If you are having a hard time with boundaries, seek support from a good friend, boss, counselor, family member, or coach whom you see as exercising their boundaries. Understand that when you know what is right or wrong (values) and you have identified what you are willing to put up with or not (boundaries), and are following them consistently, that is when you are exhibiting integrity.

LEADERSHIP EXERCISES
INTEGRITY

Leadership Exercise #5: VALUES EXERCISE

Exercise Purpose: Your values define your own personal system of what is right and wrong. This exercise is designed to help you reach a better understanding of your most significant life values as well as to build cohesiveness between people and teams by identifying and communicating the critical values that drive people.

Step 1: What I Value
From the list of values on the next page (you may consider your personal life list as well as a work leadership list), select the 12 that are most important to you as guides for how to behave, or as components of a valued way of life. Feel free to combine values or add any values of your own to this list.

Achievement	Fame	Innovation	Religion/Faith
Acceptance	Flexibility	Integrity	Reputation
Accountability	Financial growth or gain	Intellectual status	Respect
Accuracy	Forgiveness	Intimacy	Responsibility
Advancement	Freedom	Job involvement	Risk
Adventure	Friendships	Job tranquility	Peace
Affection	Fun	Knowledge	Security
Authenticity	Goal-directed	Leadership	Significance
Challenge	Growth	Learning/Education	Skillful
Collaboration	Having a family	Loving Others	Self-control
Community	Health	Loyalty	Service-oriented
Commitment	Helpful and Supportive	Meaningful work	Serenity
Communication	Helping society	Merit	Social
Competence	Honesty	Money	Solution-Oriented
Competition	Honoring	Nature	Sophistication
Compromise	Independence	Objective	Spirituality
Country	Influencing others	Orderliness	Stability
Courage	Initiative	Peace	Status
Creativity	Innovation	Persistence	Teamwork
Customer Focused	Integrity	Positive Attitude	Timeliness
Decisiveness	Intellectual status	Power and Authority	Freedom of time
Democracy	Intimacy	Privacy	Truth
Eco-friendly	Job involvement	Promotion	Trust
Effectiveness	Job tranquility	Productivity	Wealth
Efficiency	Honesty	Public service	Wisdom
Ethical practice	Honoring	Profit-oriented	Work under pressure
Excellence	Independence	Quality of work	Other:
Excitement	Influencing others	Recognition or Gratitude	Other:
Fair	Initiative		Other:

Step 2: Core Values
Now that you have identified 12 of your values, imagine that you are only permitted to have 8 values. These are the most important to you. Write your "core 8" in order of priority below.

_____   _____

_____   _____

_____   _____

_____   _____

Step 3: Clarifying Values
Knowing your values is critical. Decisions and choices come from your values. Relationships are made and broken because of differences or incompatible values. Depression, disappointment, crisis, and confusion occur when people live lives in conflict with their values. Happiness comes from being true to yourself. With this in mind, think about your top 8 values in relation to:

> Work/Career -
> Family -
> Financial -
> Social -
> Spiritual -
> Physical/Health –

Do you have any conflicting values with the expected behaviors? For example, the value of *discipline*, described as doing the same thing the same way on time every time may conflict with the value of *flexibility* which can be described as being open to new ways of doing things. This is significant because as a leader, how do people know which of your values is important at any given time, and what action should they be taking to stay in alignment with your values? Write the conflicts next to the area of your life.

<u>Questions/Points to Ponder:</u>
1. Why aren't you living consistently with your values?
2. What can you do now to make progress on acting in accordance with your values?
3. If your values were thought of as needs, are your needs getting met?

Exercise:

1. Write out a definition for each of your core values.

_____

_____

_____

2. Now write down actions and behaviors you would like to emulate that are consistent with those values.

_____

_____

_____

3. Share with someone for accountability and follow-through.

_____

_____

_____

Leadership Exercise #6: BOUNDARIES EXERCISE

Exercise Purpose: To identify your personal boundaries so that you will be seen as a decisive leader with integrity who knows when to say yes and when to say no.

Expected Outcome: To have a completed list of your personal boundaries. By writing your boundaries down, you will crystalize your thinking and be able to remind yourself when your boundaries are threatened. People will also follow you with more certainty because they know what you stand for.

Example: Before you begin filling out the Boundaries Chart on the following page, here is an explanation with examples of how to fill out the boundaries list:

Boundary Area	What is Right or Wrong	The Impact or Consequence it is Having	What I Will or Won't Accept	How I Will Communicate My Boundary
MATERIAL Determines whether you give or lend things, such as time, money, car, clothes, etc.	*My coworker keeps taking my calculator and forgets to give it back.*	*When I need it, I have to go to my coworker when he is often in a meeting with his door shut.*	*I will let people borrow some-thing once, but only if they promptly return it.*	*I will share with my coworker that he will need to get his own calculator.*
PHYSICAL Pertains to your personal space, privacy, and body.	*People in my office are all huggers, as am I, and that is comfortable.*	*We will need to make sure that hugging is acceptable for everyone else in the department.*		
MENTAL Applies to your thoughts, values, and opinions.	*Coworkers are lying about their #'s on their weekly reports to make themselves look good.*	*It has made me think that I have to do the same or else look bad in comparison.*	*I am not going to allow myself to do this anymore.*	*I will let my coworkers know that this is uncomfortable and then I will tell my boss the "what" and "why" and try to be a problem solver.*

EMOTIONAL Regarding your feelings and your responsibilities to yourself and others.	My spouse makes fun of me in front of our children and friends.	It embarrasses me. I feel unloved and belittled.	I will not let him/her do this anymore.	I will let him/her know: 1) What he/she does. 2) How it makes me feel. 3) Ask him/her to stop or tell him/her that I will leave the room if he/she does it again.

YOUR BOUNDARIES LIST

Boundary Area	What is Right or Wrong	The Impact or Consequence it is Having	What I Will or Won't Accept	How I Will Communicate My Boundary
MATERIAL Determines whether you give or lend things, such as money, car, clothes, books, food, etc.				
PHYSICAL Pertains to your personal space, privacy, and body.				
MENTAL Applies to your thoughts, values, and opinions.				
EMOTIONAL Knowing your feelings and your responsibilities to yourself and others.				

Competency Four
COMMUNICATION AND CONFLICT

In this Chapter, we will:

- Reveal communication setbacks and symptoms.

- Discuss the seven leadership communication derailers that can damage work productivity and potentially get leaders fired from their jobs.

- Give you specific ways to show up as a direct and respectful communicator.

- Teach you the six strategies for taking care of communication conflict.

- Help you identify specific conflicts in your life.

- Practice how to engage someone in a discussion during a conflict situation.

Chapter Four
COMMUNICATION AND CONFLICT

Conflict managed well builds relationships.

Communication requires a balance of listening and being able to express your thoughts, feelings, and information in a respectful manner. This is one of the earliest skills we develop as humans, and yet, astonishingly, poor communication continues to inhibit and fragment relationships, whether personal or professional.

The importance of communication is a big challenge for almost anyone. Very few individuals are master communicators. People often fail to say what they mean, whether by design, or because of fear, or because they just do not know how. They often misunderstand others, or worse, assume they understand when they don't. They respond to what is not being said, and miss what *is* said. In general, many fail to be heard, and many fail to listen.

Why do folks lack this communication awareness? Communication troubles can stem from childhood and other past experiences. We may have learned to stuff our feelings, blow up in anger, pretend we don't understand, beat around the bush, avoid confrontation, avoid looking ignorant, fear criticism... instead of just saying what we need, want or feel. Sometimes it is difficult to know what we want to say. Sometimes the act of saying it out loud can be terrifying; for others it is as simple as breathing air.

So how do you know if you have communication disconnects? Ask yourself how many of these symptoms caused by poor communication are present in your personal and professional life:

1. Unresolved conflicts in your family, your friendships, your work and life.
2. Chaos and/or confusion about the quality of your relationships – professional or personal.
3. Bottled up resentment with another person or situation.

4. Getting aggressive with your words, tone, or volume in order to get results from others.
5. Arguments or disagreements about goals and priorities.
6. People who avoid you or are brief about the information they share with you.
7. Failure to tap into the opinions and perspectives of others.
8. Wasted time and energy with posturing, trying to look good, and handling misperceptions.
9. Lack of intimacy with a loved one.
10. Failure to solicit help from peers, team members, or direct reports.
11. Telling someone repeatedly to do something, and getting no results.

If any of these symptoms exist, then it is possibly time for a communication overhaul. The good news is that communication is a skill, and therefore can be learned and improved upon. It simply involves two things—transmission and reception. A good communicator takes responsibility for both.

Effective communication involves a dialogue, and that requires active participation of two or more people. If only one person is talking in the conversation, then that is generally considered speaking, not communicating. True communication happens when both people seek to *foster understanding*.

Fostering understanding suggests that two or more people are getting their primary communication needs met, and are understanding the content being shared. When you can communicate in a way that leaves others feeling satisfied that their point of view has been understood as well as the information being shared, then you have communicated effectively.

Let's consider our reasons for communicating. We tend to communicate with ourselves (in thought) and with other people to convey a message that we have already deemed worthy of saying, most often to fill a need that we are thinking about. We communicate to give or get information. For example, we might ask someone a question because we want to know when someone will have his project done. This communication may include wanting to assist or help someone get a better result, stemming from a desire to ensure that a project gets done, or to fulfill a personal value of genuinely helping people.

For sure, there are times we need to communicate simply to vent. For example, we may want to describe our current thoughts or feelings about something or someone and still feel understood and accepted. Occasionally, further communication is needed to cause or prevent action, which may include changing or maintaining our boundaries. Ultimately, through communication, we desire to feel respected by others regardless of their age, gender, knowledge, or roles.

A frequent disconnect in communication happens when the receiver doesn't understand the content being shared. This isn't always entirely the listener's fault. So often, the communication that gets spoken is the final thought in an unspoken sequence. For example, you may say to your significant other, "I'm hungry. Let's go get a bite to eat." But that phrase was preceded by a series of thoughts that motivated the phrase to be said:

Thought One - "I am stressed out from working so much overtime and need some downtime this weekend."

Thought Two - "I might like to take a peaceful drive up to the mountains today."

Thought Three - "It might be fun to stop into that little café on the side of the mountain for breakfast."

And then we say *out loud* to our significant other, **"I'm hungry, let's go get a bite to eat."**

Then your significant other thinks:

Thought One - "Why do we have to go somewhere to eat? There is plenty of food in the refrigerator."

Thought Two – "Gosh, we are really tight on money. We are spending so much money eating out lately."

Thought Three – "We should sit down and create a financial budget."

And then your significant other says *out loud,* **"Let's eat here and spend the morning figuring out our finances."**

Now we have both parties stressed out for two very different reasons, and with both parties not getting their needs met because the communication was not effective, and clarity was not a result.

So what is the answer to this communication dilemma? Ask questions when someone makes a comment before inserting your own comment. Seek to clarify the series of thoughts that took place so you can truly understand the message being communicated. In our training sessions, we call this *listening backwards*. How do you do this? When someone makes a comment, simply ask:

"Why is that important to you?" Or....

"Will you share more?" Or....

"Why would you like to go get a bite to eat?"

There are both information and emotion involved in any communication or message, and in order to effectively communicate we must be mindful and respectful of both. We must listen backwards by asking questions.

Likewise, if the goal is to communicate your first thought, then say it. Don't say the fourth thought which is likely a morphed version of what matters and then leave the other party guessing and you wondering why you are not understood.

Communication takes all parties involved being willing to work on it. The challenge with communication is that people have different personalities, differing goals, gender and cultural differences, and preferred methods for communicating. All of these differences add up to "this is a lot of work." If a leader isn't willing to do the work necessary to achieve effective communication, his leadership suffers.

SEVEN COMMUNICATION PROBLEMS THAT CAUSE LEADERS TO "DERAIL"

In our business, we are often called into a situation where a manager or executive is *derailing*. A leader has been on the fast track to success, but something changes in the organization or with this person. The communication disconnects previously mentioned are resulting in higher employee turnover, more complaints to Human Resources, lower productivity and employee engagement, or an over-reliance on processes restricting an innovative and accountable culture. What has worked for the leader in the past, is no longer working.

We worked with a leader who had bullied his way up the ladder to VP of Operations. The owner had sold the company, and the new publicly traded parent company took over. After a year, the parent company saw that employees were resisting their processes and productivity was suffering, so they conducted an employee engagement survey. The feedback was significantly lower than any of their other divisions. And the negative feedback on this bully leader required immediate action.

The organization recognized they needed this valued employee because of his great client relationships and business knowledge of the operations, but they knew that this person would have a short future if he didn't fix his communication problems.

After we assessed the targeted individual—to understand how he was individually and naturally wired—from the perspectives of his learning abilities, personality, and interests, we began to see why specific communication problems had begun to take shape. (See page 62 in Chapter 2 Trust and Respect for the bully behaviors mentioned under False Respect.) After four team-development sessions focused on building trust, communication, and accountability, and twelve months worth of one-on-one coaching with homework exercises, the leader was back on track implementing new and practiced positive behaviors for leadership.

Invariably at the core of the derailing leader's communication problem is one of these seven issues:

1. **A leader derails if he is a "ME" monster.** Have you ever known someone who *one-ups* everything anybody says? For example, you come in to work with four inches of snow on the ground and mention that it took you forty-five minutes, and then a coworker says, "You only had four inches? That's nothing. Where I live we had eight inches and it took an hour and a half to get to work today." Or is this person possibly you?

   When I (Janet) had cancer a few years ago I called some people to let them know, and the response from most people was the same: "Oh my gosh, I am so sorry. My grandmother had colon cancer and died from it five years ago," or, "My aunt has it," or "my friend's boss," or (you fill in the blank with what you would say).

   Why do people always feel the need to jump in and steal the conversation, then tell you about themselves, who they know, or their story? Are they uncomfortable with what to say, so rather than say nothing they attach their own story to it and make it about themselves? The reason people often steal a conversation and tell you about their story is because they think they are relating.

However, what I would have appreciated the most was someone just genuinely asking me questions to understand my situation:

- *Oh my gosh! When did you find out?*
- *What are the doctors saying?*
- *What is the next step?*
- *What has been your family's reaction?*
- *What are your biggest concerns in all this?*
- *Have you gotten a second opinion?*
- *How was it diagnosed?*
- *Did you have any symptoms?*
- *Have you found an oncologist yet?*
- *Are you still continuing to work?*
- *What can I do to support you?*

And I would have appreciated them letting me tell them about my situation. That is relating. That is caring. No long story about your aunt in this situation, or how you had to trudge through the snow to get to work one day, or how your situation is so much worse, or how you have a bigger house, or a better car, or lousy job, etc.

I am now cancer free, thankfully, and more mindful of asking questions when others share their stories with me.

ME Monsters can be entertaining with their stories and they think that they are relating to you when they tell them, but most often ME Monsters are not fostering understanding in their communication because they make situations all about themselves. How can someone genuinely get to know you if they only talk about themselves and don't ask you questions?

The other thing we have noticed about ME monsters is that they will sometimes ask you a set-up question like "Are your kids in college?" as a segue for them to capture the spotlight so they can tell you about their oldest son in Law School at Harvard. They don't really care about your answer, and sometimes don't even hear it. They may as well say "Place all eyes and ears on me because I am about to tell you something that is vastly more significant than anything anybody else could possibly offer."

One time I (Ed) was talking with a friend of mine when he asked me if I ever take clients to dinner. I then shared about a client that I had taken to dinner the previous night and how my client had ordered a $200 bottle of wine with absolutely no concern about my expense budget. Rather than my friend asking a question about it, he shared how he "took a client out to dinner in Europe last year and how his client had ordered a $1,100 bottle of wine." Really? In the process of stealing the conversation, whether he meant to or not, he demonstrated that he thinks that he is more important than me. His "one-ups-manship" left me wondering if he asked me about taking clients to dinner just so that he could tell me his story. I felt set up by his question.

So how do you avoid becoming a "ME monster"? Decide to be *others-centered* in your conversations. Be intentional about asking others questions. Don't ask one question and then talk about yourself. Listen backwards. Ask multiple follow-up questions to your first question in an effort to fully understand what someone is thinking, why he thinks that way, and why it is important to him. You will always have the chance to add your story, or relate to others by sharing what you have in common with them. But get in the habit of listening to them first.

2. **Leaders derail if they are too assertive and bordering on bully behavior.** A good communicator is honest, direct, and respectful in his communication style, not pushy or aggressive. Over-assertive leaders want you to know their opinions and be impressed by their pearls of wisdom. While this can help someone get noticed, catapulting her career into management, it is the very thing that can cause her to derail. Why? Because her coworkers and employees may have learned that it is difficult to influence her, or to share a different point of view or vital but bad news. As a result, these same coworkers or employees may hesitate to give important information and withhold valuable feedback. They might feel

that they can't afford to take risks or make decisions on their own without fear of repercussions from the boss. They learn that it is unwise to disagree with the highly assertive manager and therefore tend to tell that manager only what they think she will want to hear. When a manager has a highly assertive communication style, he often ends up having a very poor perspective on how he is perceived by others in part because he tends to only respect direct and straightforward assertiveness in others. Simply, bully leaders have such admiration for their own assertiveness that they don't care how less-assertive personalities perceive them.

Bullies often bulldoze because they are secretly fearful someone will call them out on their deficiencies. So if the bully can shut others down first, motivate through fear, and shame others into doing what he demands, they won't have the chance to defend themselves. Sadly, the tyrant boss doesn't realize his inability to influence, motivate, and communicate intelligently with others. Over time this smoke screen becomes absolute truth to bullies and only to them. Sadly, bullies don't see that they are the ones who need change. It takes a 360-degree evaluation, intensive coaching and consequences before you will ever have the chance to turn them around.

How can you discern a true bully from a manager who simply needs to learn some communication skills? True bullies use "you" followed by the word "are" in their communication. For example: "You are wrong... you're stupid... you're short... you are a terrible employee... you are a rotten wife... you are dumb... you just don't get what I am talking about!" They use intimidation in their communication approach whether the approach calls for it or not, because a bully's goal is to display dominance not leadership.

3. **Leaders are susceptible to derailing if they process information fast and are educationally intelligent.** People who are smart often process quickly, so they come to conclusions faster than others, problem solve faster than others, and as a

result, the danger is to think they are better than others. They can unconsciously replace *often right* with *always right*. They unknowingly or unintentionally talk down to people when they communicate. When describing a process they think "one through ten," but what comes out of their mouth is one, four, eight, and ten in their communication. Then when the other person looks confused with the message or starts asking questions, the smart person says something like: "Never mind," or "Do you need me to detail this out for you?" Or they stop and succinctly s-p-e-l-l it all out for the other party, belittling them in the process. They might also "talk down" in their communication non-verbally. They roll their eyes or they shrug their shoulders and sigh. Smart people often think: "It's just easier to do this myself in five minutes than to take fifteen minutes to explain it." And here is the challenge, the interpretation by the person receiving the message is: "He thinks I'm dumb" or "She doesn't trust me."

If you are this smart person that we are describing, then make sure you watch out to not over-educate people. If someone that you are communicating with doesn't process as quickly, he may have tuned you out. You, the smart person, think that you have fostered understanding and the other person didn't even hear you. It is quite common for a lower assertive person who is also slower in cognitive speed to feel conflict or embarrassment with revealing that they do not understand. Their natural response is to agree, confirm that they are on track when in reality they may not have a clue as to what is being stated or asked of them. This is why a good communicator who processes information quickly takes responsibility for both the transmission and the reception of the message by:

a. Asking solid follow-up questions to confirm understanding. "Where can I offer more clarity?" or "What questions do you have back for me?"

b. Writing follow-up instructions, via memo or email, so that others are given an opportunity to read at their own speed of learning. This is particularly important for summarizing and policies, procedures, instructions, or decisions that were made in a meeting.

   c.   Asking the receiver of your message to communicate it to someone else so that you can evaluate whether they have a firm understanding of the important message.

4. **Leaders definitely derail if they are passive-aggressive.** People who are passive-aggressive have a high need to win and are very independent minded, but are not comfortable with conflict. They can deviously say the right words without any intentions of compliance. This is why you might see them go behind someone's back to get their needs met. They might use manipulation, guilt, or subtle games to get what they want. They may feel aggressive and act out of anger, but hide it under passive behaviors such as remaining silent, "forgetting" things, refusing to listen, or changing plans at the last minute.

The passive-aggressive communicator needs to recognize that when he operates this way, he shuts communication down altogether. He must learn to communicate with honesty and directness.

What the passive aggressive communicator says or does:	What the direct communicator says or does:
"Yeah, everything looks good. I am working as hard as I can." (While mentally preparing the excuse to give when the deadline is missed.)	"I am not going to be able to meet your deadline, I will need an additional three days to complete it."
(They say nothing, but schedule an appointment for 8:00 a.m. to get the person to show up on time.)	"I expect you to be at work on time at 8:00 a.m."
"Okay, I will be right there." (While thinking, I will get there when I get there.)	"Let me finish writing this proposal and I will be in your office in twenty minutes."
"Sure…let's get together to discuss it." (But thinking, "I hope that I don't have to go apologize to this customer.")	"I don't think a discussion about what to do with this customer is going to solve the problem in a timely fashion. I think we need to give our customer an apology in the next twenty-four hours."
"Do I need to stop at the grocery store on the way home tonight?"	"Would you mind making tacos for dinner tonight?"
Say nothing. Hang a dog-poop bag on the dog owners' front door after dark and hope they get the message.	"Would you mind not letting your dog poop on my lawn?"

5. **Leaders will derail if they are self-centered and unaccommodating**. Self-centered people put the needs of themselves first before the team. They are "in it to win it" people, sometimes at the expense of others. They want their goals met and don't give much credence to the consequences beyond their own circumstances. If you are self-centered and unwilling to flex to others' needs or ways of thinking, then employees, bosses, family members and friends will stop including you in on plans out of fear that you will impose your own way. They won't ask you to participate in a meeting, or a social situation that takes collaboration. Self-centered people become just another thing to have to manage, and ultimately resent and disrespect.

    Examples of these accommodating versus unaccommodating behaviors may look like:

Unaccommodating behaviors	Accommodating Behaviors
The warehouse manager tells his shipping supervisor to make the employees work Saturdays and Sundays for the next six weeks without any regard for the employees' personal lives.	The warehouse manager asks the shipping supervisor to find out how many employees would like to earn overtime pay by working weekends over the next six weeks.
The employee says she is too busy when a coworker asks for help but jumps to help an executive.	The employee recognizes the deadline-driven projects when organizing her day, but is willing to help anyone regardless of status or stature in the organization.
The CEO creates the annual strategic goals by himself and asks his direct reports what they think of them to create "buy in."	The CEO hires a facilitator for the annual meeting with key players in the organization to collaborate and create annual strategic goals.
The football coach says, "If you miss practice to go to that funeral, you won't be allowed to suit up for the game."	The football coach says, "Family is most important and you need to go to the funeral."

If you lean toward selfishness and unaccommodating tendencies, learn to say *yes* a little more often. Consider saying *yes* to the trivial, and *no* to the important. In other words, if the matter in question isn't very serious or significant, and giving the affirmative doesn't matter that much, then say *yes* whenever possible. In contrast, when the matter in question is of crucial importance with serious consequences, firmly state *no*. If you follow this guideline, then when you do say *no*, it will be respected and followed, because others know you only say *no* when absolutely necessary.

Consider the needs of others and listen to what they are saying to you.

6. **Leaders derail if they take things too personally and have difficulty staying objective**. Being objective means formulating beliefs and perceptions based on the facts in any given situation. If you are emotionally driven (you filter through feelings before facts), you have a tendency to *feel* the situation and the impact it is having on you.

So let's say someone comes to you complaining about a coworker whom you like. What happens is usually one of three things, all emotionally based:

You get defensive and shut the person down from further communicating about the situation, or...

You interpret with a feeling-based filter as to why the person is coming to you and sharing this information, then make a judgment that may or may not be accurate, or...

You say nothing, internalize the complaint, build resentment, and the other person is left wondering why you don't come around anymore.

All of these outcomes have at their core a communication problem. Emotions are individually centered and can change minute to minute. As a leader without discipline over your emotions, you may find yourself perpetually disconnected because as people work to decipher and calibrate to a current emotion, you change emotions, thus ensuring the disconnect.

I (Janet) was coaching a likeable and very bright young man, in his early thirties, who was next-in-line to take over the family-owned worldwide corporation. He mentioned that he had no relationship with his father anymore. In fact, he hadn't seen him since he was seventeen years old when his father left his mother. He talked about the impact that had on him and how he never really felt that he had someone to turn to for personal advice.

113

I asked him, "What was said or done that caused you to leave home and never talk to your father again?"

Shifting in his seat, he said, "My dad's new wife is a bitch."

I heard an interpretation on his part, not a fact. So I asked him, "What did your dad's wife say or do that caused you to believe she is a bitch?" Looking for objective evidence, I proceeded to ask him this question about three different ways.

The only objective data that he could provide was that she didn't give him keys to the house when he turned thirteen years old, and she wouldn't let him and his sister play in the living room.

I thought his perception was interesting and that there could be multiple reasons why she didn't give him keys to the house or let him play in the living room. So I asked him, "How did that make you feel when she refused to do those things?"

He replied, "I felt unloved, diminished, like I wasn't important to my dad anymore." He had interpreted his stepmother's actions without knowing her intentions, justifying his beliefs. He blamed his father for leaving his mother.

I asked him what action he took as a result of feeling diminished and unloved.

"I left home and haven't talked to my dad for sixteen years," he quietly responded.

Unfortunately, we sometimes get back at people by taking away something they want, and end up suffering the consequences ourselves.

In an effort to give him a new perspective or a different interpretation, I shared some other possibilities as to why the bitch may have done what she did. My client realized that he could no longer hold on to his story and started to see other possibilities come to light. What had been right to him was not necessarily true. He started to realize that there was a possibility that his stepmother didn't think kids were old enough at thirteen to be responsible for having keys to the house and that possibly the living room was her only sanctuary away from the chaos of the rest of the house. I asked him if this new perspective was now possibly right and true and would he have a new action that he would like to take.

To this day, his answer makes me emotional when I think about it.

He answered, "Yes, I would like to go call my dad right now if that is okay."

Just as with this client, many of us often judge others based upon their actions, and only ourselves on our intentions. For example, if a coworker comes walking into a meeting late, I might judge her for not having control over her time. But if I am the one late for a meeting, it's certainly not because I didn't intend to get there on time. It was because something else happened. My standard for timeliness is based on my *intention* to be timely and I see your standard of timeliness based on your *actions* to be timely, in which case you failed.

This kind of "my intentions vs. your actions" behavior happens daily. In traffic, when another driver cuts me off, I gripe that the idiot did it on purpose. But had I sped into traffic in the same reckless maneuver, for sure I would have had a legitimate reason for it. I didn't have room to slow down or I was avoiding a rabbit. But in all truth, perhaps the idiot didn't see me, or he was rushing to the hospital, or screaming kids in the back seat were causing a distraction. If the rules of the road were consistent with actions vs. actions, we could all admit to a time when our driving skills imposed danger on another driver. Only the individual knows his own intentions. If we try to interpret someone's intentions based only on his actions, we're missing an important part of communication.

If you have a conflict with someone in your life—a coworker, boss, employee, friend, sibling, parent, or child—call that person or meet with them, and use the following technique:

1. Go to the person and check it out. "*Can I check something out with you?*"
2. Describe the situation or behavior as you have observed it. Say something like: "*When you didn't invite me to the meeting...*"
3. Explain how you interpreted it or how it made you feel. Say something like: "*...it made me think that you didn't want me there for a reason.*"
4. Then to gain clarity ask if that is what they meant to say or do. "*Is that what you meant to communicate or do?*"

What you are trying to do is to foster understanding because clarity is infinitely more valuable that being right. Be prepared, however, to listen, and sincerely try to understand it from their perspective.

5. **Leaders derail when they avoid conflict.** Avoiding conflict can be tantamount to kicking the solution can down the road. Avoidance causes delay of a positive resolution, and by the time the conflict absolutely must be dealt with, it is now bigger, more volatile, and much more personal than had it been handled at the first opportunity. When people avoid conflicts, they start to build resentment. Resentment leads to bitterness, self-pity, and loss of productivity.

   Sometimes people avoid conflict because they don't like the feelings associated with it. But when an individual allows personal emotions to take priority over pursuing a better result, this becomes a self-centered position. To make matters worse, a leader who avoids conflict or keeps the peace can actually teach others how to manipulate him. Because they know he won't resist or confront them, they've learned to get stern to get him to acquiesce, and they get what they want and often at his expense.

   Another reason leaders may avoid conflict is because they are not in touch with their personal or business values. If they were aware of their values, they could leverage them by using them as the reason for engaging in conflict. For example, a leader is in a meeting where one of his coworkers is promoting an idea. The leader has vital information that suggests the idea won't work, but he doesn't want to make his coworker look bad. As a result, the leader withholds opposing information that could set the team in the right direction. If this leader had identified his values of honesty and reliability, and had given them priority, he would have a defined and purposeful reason to engage in the conflict.

   People with good communication skills are willing to engage in disagreements and point out discrepancies in others or situations, so undoubtedly good communicators will experience conflict. When conflicts arise and two people are committed to a win/win outcome, they recognize that the only way to keep the relationship strong is to share and listen to each other's point of view. It is essential to distinguish productive conflict from destructive fighting. Productive conflict is limited to concepts and ideas, and avoids the destruction that occurs from personally attacking another's personality, abilities, or values.

So why are some people uncomfortable with conflict? It may have to do with their personality, their past experiences, their values, fear of a potential outcome, or simply lack of skills to handle it. Whatever the reason, avoiding conflict keeps people from having productive communication or intimate relationships. When conflicts are avoided, opportunities to learn and mature are thwarted, and relationships remain undeveloped. On the other hand, vast learning occurs in the process of dealing with and overcoming conflicts.

When we think back on family situations when there has been conflict, it is those situations that bring the family closer. Think about camping. Something seems to always go wrong along the way—somebody forgets the tent, the RV breaks down, shoes didn't get packed for the kids, the weather turns cold and miserable, etc. When a family jumps in together to solve a problem—scrounge for more blankets, create makeshift shoes from the cereal box—they are handling conflict together, and that builds relationships.

Changing your mindset to become more conflict-engaged after a lifetime of avoidance is more than a simple decision. Recognize the way you react in a conflict situation, then ask yourself, "Is this the way that I want to respond?" or "Am I making this response about my feelings?" And remember: The *way you act* often affects the *way others react* to *you*.

STRATEGIES FOR HANDLING CONFLICT

Here are a few tips for handling conflict that will help you in your personal and professional life:

1. **Accept the fact that conflict is going to happen in any relationship where there is communication.** Decide to take positive steps to manage it. When it occurs, discuss the conflict openly with the person or group of people because there

might be an improved result.

> *"There seems to be more than one way to view this situation. May I give you a different perspective?"*

2. **Choose the right time for the conflict.** Individuals have to be willing to address the conflict and be in the right frame of mind. If someone is overwhelmed in her workload, discussing a conflict situation may have a better result if left for a less congested date.

> *"Is this a good time to talk about our conversation that we had yesterday?"*

3. **Avoid using and/or reacting to unintentional remarks.** Words like "always" and "never" may be said in the heat of battle but do not necessarily convey what the speaker means. Anger will escalate the conflict rather than bring it closer to resolution. It's like the manager who has an employee who has been late to work on three separate occasions in the last two weeks. Recognizing he needs to address the behavior, the manager says to the employee, "You are always late!" The result of the manager phrasing it this way is that the manager and employee end up arguing over the word "always" and don't get to the solution of how the employee can get to work on time. Be sure to stick to the specifics.

DON'T SAY	DO SAY
"This report is totally unacceptable."	"There are three changes that I would like to see in this report…"
"You never check your work for mistakes before submitting it to management."	"I have noticed mistakes on the last two reports that you have submitted to management. Are you checking your work first?"
"Why am I always the one having to stay late to get the department's projects done?"	"I have noticed in the last month, that I have had to work overtime on six separate occasions to get the department's projects completed. How do you see it? Is there anything that I should be doing differently?"

4. **Avoid name-calling and threatening behavior.** Don't corner a coworker, literally and figuratively. All parties need to preserve their dignity and self-respect. Threats usually increase the conflict and tear down relationships and always at the cost of the organization. When people are genuinely fearful, they might lash out at others. Instead, we have a phrase in our organization that we sometimes say to ourselves when we are nervous, scared, stressed, or mad. We say, "Just be the duck on the pond." A duck gliding across a glassy pond looks so in control, peaceful, smooth, and calm. But under the surface of the pond the duck's little legs are paddling a mile a minute. You can feel the frustration and acknowledge the anger to yourself privately, but don't show that level of emotion to the other person. Reduce the emotion and communicate the issue calmly without exaggeration.

5. **Don't insist on being right.** There are usually several right solutions to every problem. Coming across as if you are the only one with answers will send someone in the relationship packing faster than anything else; it suggests that there is no room for another perspective in the room. A friend of ours often says about relationships… "If one of you in the relationship is the only one with all the right answers, then there would be no need for a relationship, now would there?"

6. **Offer and accept apologies without hesitation.** Too often apologies are given or received with little sincerity, or they are a clever way to communicate a disguised message. When accepting an apology, avoid adding any judgment to it. (For more on apologies, see Chapter Two: Trust and Respect.)

The key ingredient to great communication in relationships is to maintain the self-esteem of others. Positive, affirming behaviors go a long way toward establishing effective interactions. Consider the empowering impact when members of a tennis team cheer on their comrade. "You got this, girl! Just hit it like you did last time," hailed onto the tennis court inspires the tired player to keep going. It also inspires her to return the encouragement to her teammates when it is their turn to take to the courts.

Remind others that they are valuable to you and the organization. Catch people doing things right. Point out specific things that you like, and tell them why you like it. It makes your communication more sincere.

The more positive comments you invest through good communication into a relationship, whether personal or professional, the more confident and connected the relationship will be. Then, when you find yourself in a conflict situation, the relationship will be solid enough to work through it to reach a favorable solution. Exercising your communication and managing conflict in leadership will yield tremendous growth—in your relationships and your career.

ADVICE FROM YOUR COACH

Choose to see conflict as a conversation. When you avoid conflict, you build resentment, which can lead to a bitter heart and little opportunity for mended relationships. So embrace conflict and see it as an opportunity to build trust and improved relationships in your personal and professional life.

LEADERSHIP EXERCISES
COMMUNICATION
AND CONFLICT

Leadership Exercise #7: INTERPRETATION EXERCISE

Exercise Purpose: Build better relationships by changing the base of a person's belief from interpretation to facts.

Expected Outcome: A renewed motivation and plan to respectfully confront a person you have conflict with.

Basic human nature drives people to understand meaning, to answer the question *why?* If this meaning is not understood, the imperfect human will make up what he feels is the most likely reason to fill the gap, and this interpreted meaning is not always accurate. Yet it has a significant impact on a relationship, both good and bad.

The interpretation process unfolds as follows. Something is said or done – this leads to an interpretation – which motivates a feeling – which inspires an action. Actions are based on interpretations. These interpretations are often wrong and misleading so the ensuing action is wrong and misleading. The following diagram outlines an example of the interpretation process and how to fill out the questions in the chart.

1.	How did the conflict originate? What was the situation that happened when the conflict started with this person? *I was purposely not invited by my coworker to a meeting that I should have been in. Now I have lots of questions as to why people have decided to use this web design approach.*
2.	What was "said" or "done" that caused you to feel the conflict? List only the facts. (Example: "She told me that my blouse reminded her of her grandmother" – is the fact. Do not list your interpretation of the facts. "She thinks I dress like an old lady" is an interpretation.) *I was not on the email invitation to the meeting so I did not know about it and couldn't attend.*

3.	How did it make you feel when the other person "said" or "did" that? *I felt like I was purposely left out of the meeting because they weren't interested in my ideas. It made me feel disrespected and devalued.*
4.	What action did you take, or what did you say when the other person behaved the way that he/she did? Did your action help or hinder the development of a relationship? *I sent my coworker an email that she should have included me in the meeting. I have also decided that I won't invite her to the leadership training we are offering because I don't want to be in the same meeting as her.*
5.	Now consider the other possibilities by asking yourself questions like: Imagine that you are coaching someone else. What other possibilities could there be for that person's behavior? If you were to give them the benefit of the doubt, why do you think they said or did that? *Maybe she really didn't mean to exclude me from the email.* *Maybe I talk too much in meetings, and she didn't want me to dominate the conversation.*
6.	Do you have a new perspective? If not, what will you lose by continuing to hold onto your belief or opinion of the person? Are you able to forgive? If you can't, what will that cost you? *I can try to believe that she didn't intentionally leave me out of the meeting because, if I don't, both of us will lose from not being in on things.*
7.	Consider going to the person and checking it out with them, and don't be afraid to learn that your interpretation was wrong. a. Say: "Can I check something out with you?" b. Say: "When you (describe what was said or done). c. Say: "It made me feel/think (describe how their action or words made you feel or what it made you think). d. Ask: "Is that what you meant?"

And listen to his/her perspective. Stay open to a differing point of view. You may learn something!

Consider the people in your life whom you have the most conflict with. With each conflict situation answer the following series of questions:

1.	How did the conflict originate? What was the situation that happened when the conflict started with this person?
2.	What was "said" or "done" that caused you to feel the conflict? List only the facts.
3.	How did it make you feel when the other person "said" or "did" that?
4.	What action did you take, or what did you say when the other person behaved the way that he/she did? Did your action help or hinder the development of a relationship?
5.	Now consider the other possibilities by asking reframing questions. Imagine that you are coaching someone else. What other possibilities could there be for his/her behavior? If you were to give him/her the benefit of the doubt, why do you think he/she said or did that?

6.	Do you have a new perspective? If not, what will you lose by continuing to hold onto your belief or opinion of the person? Are you able to forgive? If you can't, what will that cost you?

7.	Consider going to the person and "checking it out" with him/her, and don't be afraid to learn that your interpretation was wrong.
	
	  a. Say: "Can I check something out with you?"
	
	  b. Say: "When you (describe what was said or done).
	
	  c. Say: "It made me feel/think (describe how their action or words made you feel or what it made you think).
	
	  d. Ask: "Is that what you meant?"

And listen to his/her perspective. Stay open to a differing point of view. You may learn something!

Competency Five
ACCOUNTABILITY

In this Chapter, we will:

- Teach you how to understand the difference between excuses and real reasons.

- Help you recognize when you are using victim language that causes others to lose respect for you as a leader.

- Give you seven strategies for becoming more accountable.

- Practice replacing *blaming* statements with *accountable* statements.

Chapter Five
ACCOUNTABILITY

*Victim mindsets look back and ask why and who. Accountable people
look forward and ask what and how.*

You may be familiar with the old story by an anonymous author about four characters named Everybody, Somebody, Anybody, and Nobody. There was an important job to be done and Everybody was asked to do it. Everybody thought Anybody could do it and was sure that Somebody would do it. Somebody got angry because it was Everybody's job. Anybody could have done it, but Nobody did it. It ended that Everybody blamed Somebody when Nobody did what Anybody could have done.

Accountability is all about taking the initiative to accept responsibility for something and doing what it takes to make it happen. Unaccountable people don't take initiative; they wait for others to take action or tell them what to do.

Accountability can often be seen as a word with negative consequences such as "Who should we blame if something is not done." But accountability in the context of leadership refers to the willingness to embrace responsibility, following through on commitments, and the relentless pursuit of personal, team, and organizational goals.

This goes beyond accepting the responsibilities that are handed to you. A motivated leader steps forward and volunteers, "I want to do that too!" For example, a young couple may learn a baby is on the way and accept the responsibility that goes with being parents. But if they *embrace* parenthood, they will take parenting classes, identify their parenting standards, observe experienced parents, and check in with each other continually to ensure they are abiding by their agreed upon list of values. And both new mommy and daddy are committed to their fair share of the parenting deal.

Throughout our years as leadership coaches, we have seen a huge difference between the responsible, accountable leader and the one who gets by with as little effort as possible, willing to sit back and watch others carry the load. These differences are especially notice-able whenever a problem or a mistake has occurred. Accountable leaders tend to position problems as a means to learn and clarify, and they spend very little energy and time beating people up for mistakes. They are quick to find solutions because their gratification comes not in identifying who is at fault, but in achieving a result. Backseat leaders, however, continue to point the blame finger rather than assume responsibility to make things better. They abide by the philosophy: It's easier to say something is not your fault, or make excuses, than it is to accept responsibility. (Incidentally, those who blame the most are also the most sensitive about being the target of blame, so if you are instinctively maneuvering to avoid blame, you may want to examine this chapter closely.)

Unfortunately, sometimes a persuasive excuse can almost pass as a result. For example, an employee may use this excuse for missing a project deadline: "Another project came up that you said was a more important priority, so I assumed that this project was less import-ant." The employee hopes the boss will accept the blame, admitting that he actually is at fault for requesting such a high demand task. But how does this excuse really make the employee look? Lazy? Disrespectful? Dishonest? Manipulative? Hopefully the discerning boss will recognize that the employee is simply using an excuse to avoid being responsible.

Consider the following excuses and ask yourself if you have ever used them to avoid being responsible for something in your child-hood, relationships, school, or work life:

"It's not my fault."
"I didn't know that you needed it right away."
"If you would have told me that it was important to you, then I would have done it."
"She's the one who shared the secret first."
"It's (someone else's) fault."
"I didn't want to bother them." (Implying it is to somebody else's benefit that you didn't communicate because you are super con-siderate and such a great person.)
"I don't have my workout clothes with me."
"Why didn't you tell me?"

"I thought you were going to handle it." (You might ask, "But what if I thought someone else *was* going to handle it? It's not my fault that the job didn't get done." Well, did you consider following up with the person who you thought was going to handle it? If you know full well that your contribution to a project is due four days ahead of a deadline even though nobody told you directly, then you are accountable to reverse the communication flow and go check in, not sit there and wonder when you will receive confirmation on dates.)

In those times when you are connected to a situation that has gone wrong, do you cast blame or make an excuse, or do you acknowledge your part in the mishap? Sometimes there is a legitimate reason for executing poorly. The difference between an excuse and a reason is whether you are looking at the situation from a past perspective and explaining to someone why something wasn't done or a future perspective where you anticipate potential problems and take action so that you aren't left having to give an excuse.

- Past perspective means that someone is asking you why the execution was poor, and your response blames someone or something else – "I was waiting for approval from my boss, so I had very little time to get the project done."
- Future perspective means that you recognize that execution will be poor if you don't get fast approval from your boss (reason), giving yourself enough time to get the project done.

Unaccountable people tend to look back and ask why and who, whereas responsible people look forward and ask what and how. One is always better off admitting the mistake and moving toward a solution. Consider the situation as a problem to be solved rather than a responsibility to avoid by uttering excuses.

You may not realize that when others hear you repeating excuses, people don't believe they can count on you. Imagine an absentee father committing to his son every summer to take him to Disneyland, and never following through. And who tells his son on the phone year after year that he put a birthday card or a present in the mail, only for it to never show up. The child begins, with good reason, to doubt his father's words. Eventually the child stops listening.

Consider the person who repeatedly bumps into you at the grocery store or at work and says, "We should have you guys over for dinner to our house sometime." After about the fifth time you have heard this, what becomes your perception of them? That they are all talk and no action? That they don't really mean it? That what they say can't be relied on? Bottom line: Don't commit to something, unless you are going to act upon it.

Taking responsibility for your actions, your life, and your attitude is the difference between contentment and resentment. If you believe someone else is responsible for your happiness, you will be disappointed and ultimately resentful because it just doesn't work that way. When you retain the belief that someone else has to change in order for you to be happy, be prepared for happiness to never materialize because however many changes are made, there is always one more change to make. Ask yourself what change you are willing to make instead. Look at your less-than-favorable situation and ask yourself the accountability question – *What else can I do to get better results?* Then act upon the idea, and you will experience the joy and contentment that accompany knowing you did everything possible to make a difference to improve the outcome.

By the time I (Janet) was nineteen years old, I had already been married, divorced, and was raising a son alone. The massive responsibility of my plight was huge. I was earning $850 per month in a clerical/administrative position. With $260 per month for the babysitter and $425 per month for rent, I had little left over to pay for living expenses like groceries or diapers. I would even coast down hills in my run-down car to conserve on gas.

On this particular day, it was 8:00 a.m. and I was sitting at my desk when the phone rang. I answered to hear my ex-husband of ten months inform me that, once again, I would not be receiving any child support. The court had ruled that he provide me and the baby with $250 per month. That $250 was critical to our basic survival.

After I hung up the phone, I sat staring at the wall in despair. Just then my boss, Bill, walked through the door to start his day at work. He could tell that something was wrong, so he invited me into his office to talk.

I spilled my sad victim story for at least forty-five minutes while Bill just listened. When I was finally exhausted from talking and felt that he understood my situation, I asked him what I should do.

The message of accountability that he shared changed the direc-

tion of my life.

*His response went something like this... "I am so sorry to hear that you have all of this weight on your shoulders. No one your age should have to go through this." He empathized with me and validated the difficulty of my circumstances, and then he spoke what would be literally life-altering words. "**Sometimes what we have to do in life is stop looking at what we don't have, and start looking at what we need, and then plan for how we are going to get it.**"*

I realized in that moment that I had to figure out how to make an extra $250 per month...or more. I realized that I was continuing to fall victim to my ex-husband's abuse because I was allowing it. I was unsuccessful at turning lemons into lemonade (even with the court's help), so I had to try something different.

That week I borrowed $4.75 from my parents to purchase a calligraphy book. I spent the evenings after Chris went to sleep practicing this craft until I was good enough to put together a portfolio of my sample work. I then went to print shops on the weekends to sell my calligraphy services (while I hate to admit this because it reveals my age, back then word-processors were just being introduced so customers still ordered wedding invitations in personalized calligraphy). Interestingly enough, I started averaging an extra income of... $250 per month.

The next eighteen months were still a considerable struggle, but at the age of twenty-one I began to recognize my natural ability to sell. So I convinced my boss to put me into a sales position for the company. This catapulted my career. By the time I was twenty-seven years old, I was earning a six-figure income, dwarfing the $250 monthly maintenance. It all started because I took responsibility for my own situation rather than acting like a victim.

It is critical to recognize that there are true and unfortunate circumstances when people truly are victims. Some people have mental and physical disabilities that keep them from being able to care for themselves. Others suffer at the hand of people who don't care if they cause harm. Due to an unfair world that we can't control, we may find ourselves looking up at the underside of the bus we've been thrown under, or fall victim to theft or personal harm. These are circumstances when, through no fault of our own, we become true victims.

Accountable people are able to bounce back from defeat, setbacks, or adversity and continue moving toward goals, rather than surrendering to despair. Imagine that you are on a race team or departmental team, and others are counting on you to finish the race, but you allow past hurts to control your response. Have you ever heard yourself say:

- "I just don't have the ability to figure this out, someone else needs to handle this."
- "There is no way that I can meet this deadline."
- "This is probably just a waste of effort."
- "Nobody listens to me anyway."

These comments reflect a defeated attitude of a victim who has been beaten down, and stayed down. Accountable people muster the desire and perseverance to get back up, figure things out. Those who remain stuck as victims, whether real or imaginary, and nurse their wounded pride indefinitely, become *false victims*.

In one of our training programs, we show how people can identify when they are acting like false victims. Jeff Foxworthy, the famous comedian, is known for coining the phrase "you know you're a redneck if…." We applied that same process to being a false victim. Have fun reviewing some of the following possible scenarios to see if you think or act like a victim, understanding that we really mean false victim.

1. If you repeatedly describe a bad experience to as many people as you can because you want them to know how tough and unfair your life is…you might be a victim.
2. If it makes you feel better to share a current problem that you are personally experiencing with somebody you just met… you might be a victim.
3. If you hear a problem that somebody else is facing or had to endure, and you "one-up" them so they know that your life is worse… you might be a victim.
4. If a minor health problem like a cold or a bruise ruins your entire week… you might be a victim.
5. If you look for opportunities to get other people in trouble and justify it as being the right thing to do… you might be a victim.
6. If problems in your life keep repeating themselves, such as

relationship turnovers, repeatedly quitting jobs, or moving residences every year... you might be a victim.

7. If you avoid seeking feedback from others on how you can improve because you are afraid of what they will say... you might be a victim.

8. If you find yourself saying "They don't understand my situation" more than once a month ... you might be a victim.

9. If you feel like someone owes you an apology more than once a month... you might be a victim.

10. If you get fired from a job more than once, and blame anyone else but yourself... you might be a victim.

11. If you find yourself using phrases like "that's how my life seems to be," or "I get blamed once again," or "my friends never invite me out," or "it's not my fault"... you might be a victim.

12. If the most common phrases in your vocabulary are "Why do I have to do it all?" or "Why is it always my job?" or "No one seems to help around here"... you might be a victim.

13. If you exaggerate and overuse words like "always," "never," and "every time," when they really don't accurately describe something... you might be a victim.

14. If bending the truth doesn't feel weird or wrong anymore... you are definitely a victim.

15. If you have a voice in your head or a loop that constantly plays in the silence of your mind about how you were treated unfairly... you are also a victim.

And one more thought to consider: You may be a false victim if you can't immediately think of a time when you caused strife in somebody else's life. The idea is this... In the pursuit of individual needs, others' needs are at times overlooked or violated. It could be as simple as a last minute decision to change lanes while driving thus causing another driver to slam on her brakes. Or perhaps going around your boss to get approval or phoning your spouse at work five times a day just because you're bored. If you are not willing to admit that you have done something that imposed a negative effect on another person, then the hard truth is you are not taking responsibility for your actions and the impact that it has on others.

Our redneck list of false victim characteristics may seem funny, but in actuality, there's nothing funny about a person stuck in the mindset of being a victim. He is holding his own life back by not accepting the responsibility to change his situation.

When a person remains trapped as a victim, he develops victim behavior. One sign of victim behavior is blaming others, as real and as justified as it may seem at times. Those who exhibit victim behavior often operate with an entitled attitude. They ironically find energy and purpose in ruining other people's day and in the process make themselves look bad.

I (Janet) drove into the parking lot of a local restaurant where I was meeting a group of women to discuss a sales opportunity. We were meeting for lunch and there were going to be eight of us. I saw that there were two parking spaces available near the front door, except that one car on the left was parked over the line, really only leaving one good spot on the right. So I took it. I turned off my car, but sat there for a few minutes finishing up a conversation on my cell phone.

Suddenly I heard someone laying on the horn, certainly trying to get someone's attention. I turned around and the woman who was honking started to yell at me. She shouted that I did not leave her enough room in the other parking spot, that she has a baby and needs to be parked near the front.

Reacting a little in disbelief at her entitlement, I genuinely responded, "If it will help you, I will back my car out of my spot and go find a new spot, then you can have this one." She scoffed at my calm demeanor and drove off like a mad woman to find another spot.

After I finished my call, I went inside for the meeting and sat down with the other six women who were already there. Lo and behold, who comes walking up to the table as the eighth person but the livid, horn-honking, mad woman.

As she took her seat, I thought I am really glad that I was nice. I don't know what she was thinking, but I can't believe she felt very good about herself at the moment.

The first step in overcoming victim behavior is to accept the fact life isn't designed to be fair. Every human on the planet encounters unfairness regularly. So what right does any individual have to complain about it? The beauty is that your purpose for living can thrive with meaning and prosper in an unfair world. Fairness is a choice and is within your control. Be fair to yourself by choosing to make things happen instead of watching things happen to you.

> **Joy and fulfillment in life are not determined on "the fair to unfair continuum." This is the wrong scale and the wrong measure. Those who are focused on what is fair tend to only see the unfair, so their level of unfairness is always greater. By continuously focusing on your own personal needs, you miss the joy and personal growth that can be experienced by meeting the needs of another. Joy and fulfillment come by stepping out of self-centeredness and into being others-centered.**

This means accommodating other people's needs and goals regardless of your measure of necessity or ability. It's a willingness on your part to go help a friend instead of clean your own house. It's pitching in to help a coworker complete a project so that the whole team can go home on time, instead of looking at your job as finished and it's their problem that they can't work as fast as you do. It's letting go of the anger associated with someone taking *your* parking spot, instead of cursing at them.

Accountable leaders recognize that what motivates others is positive recognition, feedback, praise or a demonstrated belief on your part in their ability to accomplish a goal or meet an expectation.

STRATEGIES TO OVERCOME THE VICTIM MINDSET

If your goal is to become a more responsible and accountable leader, consider putting these actions in your life:

1. **Take responsibility for every choice, decision, and action without blaming others**. Wear a rubber band around your wrist and the next time you catch yourself blaming someone or something, snap the rubber band. While this sounds hokey, this habit may help you stop. Taking ownership leads to results, contentment, and success, and ultimately that is what is fair.

2. **Make a plan, verify that it is realistic, and tell others what you want to achieve and what you will do to achieve it.** A public declaration has a better chance of succeeding. If you tell your friends that you are going on a diet and your goal is to lose twenty pounds, then you are engaging partners to help hold you accountable. Accountability partners can help you stay true to your goal if you give them permission to speak frankly when you drift from your goal.

3. **Invite feedback from others on your performance, character, or behaviors.**
   Victims solicit sympathy. Accountable leaders solicit feedback! Ask your friends, family, coworkers, boss, or members of the community how they perceive you being accountable to the job or relationship and where you could improve. Consider these three accountability audit questions:

   a. What else can I do to contribute more to the success of the team?

   b. Do I exhibit specific behaviors that hinder the team or individual players from performing their job effectively? What are they? What can I do different?

   c. Where can I be more responsive to the team? How quickly do I follow up? Does the team often wait on me for decisions, plans, etc.?

   The challenge with asking for feedback comes in how you handle the feedback that comes your way. One indicator of accountability is revealed in your response when the feedback is negative. Victims argue or justify negative feedback, and accountable leaders ask questions for clarity. Take a minute to remind yourself of your most recent negative feedback. How did you naturally react?

   We have had coaching clients say to us, "I have stopped giving him feedback because all we do is get into an argument about how he is right and I am wrong. So why bother giving any?" This is what may happen if you do not gracefully say something like, "Thank you for the feedback. May I ask you some questions to better understand the specific behaviors that I need to change?" When people care enough about us to deliver feedback that may hurt initially but help us in the long run, we need to care about them enough to avoid shutting them down or denouncing the feedback.

Yes, negative feedback can be hard to hear, but it is worse to go through life without it, only to find out later in life that your opportunities were limited because of things you didn't know about yourself.

4. **Be proactive, rather than reactive.** Will you be someone who waits for things to happen, or will you make things happen? Being proactive requires a commitment to planning your goals out so you can move forward with a purpose. It means identifying the obstacles to your goals (the things that could go wrong), and brainstorming solutions so that your obstacles don't become the twenty-foot block wall that keeps you from your goals, rather than the speed bump on the road to your success.

I (Janet) left my job as a Vice President of Sales to start up my own training and development company, The Employers Edge, in 1991. During my first year as a new business owner I learned how difficult it was to stay proactive. I hadn't realized up until that point that work had been easier with project deadlines to meet, meetings to attend, and other people demanding my time and attention. In my previous job, all I needed to do was react to the expectations and responsibilities that had been set in place for me.

So, here I was, out on my own, with no determined time- or people-demands. I had to self-inspire the motivation to cold call companies that had no idea who I was. I had to create my own marketing materials, website, bookkeeping, and training materials. The challenge wasn't really learning to do all of this as much as mastering the mindset of self-inspiration. The challenge was not having a boss to demand I get something done, or a paycheck that guilted me into being productive. Now with my own business, getting something done became my choice.

What I really learned was how to be accountable to myself because I had a purpose to move towards. I had to create my own version of a boss. In a way, my purpose became my boss that I had to answer to. I created a business plan, life plan, and created goal project plan-

ning worksheets (See Chapter 7 on Future Focus - Exercise #11) that helped me figure out what actions and target dates needed to be achieved in order to get results.

With responsibility comes action, and with action comes commitment and hard work. At the end of the day, week, month, year or your life, ensure that the examples of life you reflect back on are worthy of pride and tell a story of truth and accountability.

ADVICE FROM YOUR COACH

Take responsibility for your mistakes and don't commit to things unless you are going to act upon it. People will trust you more in the long run. And remember, there is not a single human being who is perfect. In fact, people don't trust perfect people…they think that they are hiding something. So just go be your responsible self!

LEADERSHIP EXERCISES
ACCOUNTABILITY

Leadership Exercise #8: THE BLAME GAME

Exercise Purpose: To recognize and eliminate blaming language, mindset, and behaviors.

Expected Outcome: When you have completed this exercise, you should be able to look at yourself and recognize that you, like others, sometimes use excuses to avoid being responsible for something. When you have identified excuses that you or others use, make sure you put time into thinking through another more accountable way to act.

Think of a time when you avoided being responsible for something. Perhaps you blamed someone else? What was the situation? What would you have done differently if you were more accountable?

_____

_____

_____

Write down three goals that you are responsible for accomplishing in the next six months:

_____

_____

_____

Now imagine that it is six months from today and you haven't come close to accomplishing one of your goals listed above. You've been asked for an explanation for why you haven't reached those goals. Now, write down below the excuses you would use if you were acting like a blaming victim. Use victim language like "It's someone else's fault, I didn't think that goal was important anymore, etc." What excuses might you come up with? List them below:

_____

_____

_____

_____

_____

_____
_____
_____
_____
_____

Do you sense that some of these excuses aren't really excuses, but have a fair amount of truth behind them and they really do cause performance delays? For example, there is a legitimate, often arduous, red tape process to getting new computers approved, the sales force is unresponsive, or perhaps a software has bugs and keeps crashing the system. Understand these are still excuses because they motivate a trapped and stifled mindset.

Now that you have thought of the excuses you might use, think of accountable statements that you can use instead. In the chart on the next page, you will see some examples of blaming victim statements, and opposite those is a more accountable way to look at the situation with a more accountable statement. When you have looked over the examples, add some excuses that you have heard from others, and see if you can think of a more accountable way to say it.

Blaming Victim Statement	Accountable Statement
"I am not going to be able to sell anything because my customer called and said that he is on credit hold."	"Let me better understand why my customer is on credit hold and see if I can help the situation. In the meantime, I will contact non-active customers to see if I can generate additional business."
"I am waiting for approval from my boss."	"I will email or text my boss to let her know that I need to get approval in the next four hours in order to meet the project deadline. In the meantime, I will review my work to ensure there are no mistakes."

Blaming Victim Statement	Accountable Statement

Competency Six
INFLUENCE

In this Chapter, we will:

- Identify the keys to leadership influence.
- Discover the three types of motivation—which ones work and which ones don't.
- Discuss influential coaching.
- Learn the seven appreciation styles and how to encourage people based upon their appreciation style.
- Explore what to say and do to spark enthusiasm.
- Teach the three-step formula for giving others positive appreciation and praise.

Chapter Six
INFLUENCE

Positive feedback reinforces positive behavior.

For fifteen years, the popular reality television show American Idol dominated the networks. Vocalists auditioned before a panel of scrutinizing judges in hopes of earning a spot in the national competition, perhaps even winning the coveted title of American Idol. Viewers across the nation watched and listened as contestants, some with amazing talent, entered into the initial rounds of American Idol. Several successful artists can attribute the launch of their careers back to this highly viewed show.

Occasionally there were contestants who believed they were tremendously talented artists, but listening to them sing was brutal. They would walk onto the platform and belt out a song in the form of screeches and whines, but what they heard in themselves was pure elegance and beauty. When the judges asked them how they felt their performance went, they'd answer confidently, often saying, "This is what I was born to do. Singing means everything to me." They most likely practiced their performance in front of the mirror a hundred times and never picked up on the problems of their musical shortfalls. How they saw their performance in comparison to how the judges and the public viewed it was in itself entertaining, while sad at the same time. We call this The American Idol Effect.

When interviewed, many of the Idol contestants expressed that their family, friends, and associates in their circle have told them for years how good they are. What they don't know is that their circle didn't have the heart to tell them their talent needs work. Intentions to spare someone's feelings are noble, but the destruction of telling somebody that they are good at something that they are not is a life-size disservice. This is not to be confused with declaring someone can't do it or will never make it. That is equally destructive. But to repeatedly influence a person into believing she has a current skill level that she does not possess is to mislead and misguide her, setting her up for unavoidable disaster. An effective leader needs to learn the skill of how to lead honestly and effectively through the power of influence.

What is influence? Influence is the capacity to have an effect on the character, development, or behavior of someone or something. Influential leaders show people the possibilities of how things can be and encourage people to try new things, all the while instilling in them the benefits of being included. In other words, influential leaders are filled with personal enthusiasm for helping people, specifically to help them grow and change. Positive influential leaders are willing to develop the skill to create vision and purpose as well as coach and motivate others to take action on their goals. They help others become self-aware, and how to build on their strengths and manage their weaknesses.

Becoming an influential leader in all aspects of your life requires a commitment to exercising the main elements to be a positive influence: Coaching, Motivating, Vision Defining, and Enthusiasm.

Coaching

In the area of influence, where the value comes increasingly from the knowledge of people, the necessity for the leader as a coach emerges. There is more to coaching than just revealing a person's shortcomings, as evidenced by one of the infamous coaches on American Idol. Simon, seemingly heartless at times, had the courage to tell participants the truth about their abysmal singing, but he also crushed hopes and dreams in the process. Highly assertive contestants got angry and fought back, and highly emotional contestants fell apart in tears. Both of these responses left the contestants stifled in their boots, and neither left the contestants motivated to explore a path that some truly did have a talent for. Simon's feedback of "that was the most atrocious performance I have ever witnessed" may have been true and it's about time the truth was said, but it did not offer direction as to how to improve or how to explore another talent. It did not move the contestant down a path of better performance, and as a result, the best opportunity for positively influencing that contestant was lost.

Simon had the courage to deliver the hard news but some say that he took it too far and crossed the line into being known for getting his energy from being hard core. It became about *him*, not developing, guiding, or mentoring a contestant. Leaders have been known to follow the same progression. They begin courageously delivering the hard news and over time they cross the line; they taste the blood of delivering the hard news and begin to absorb energy from it. It becomes them, it evolves into an identity and the leadership position is reduced to a title only, and not in the transfer of wisdom.

The production of a television show doesn't allow for discovery, but a good coach will. Herein lies the value of a leader who fully understands the role and responsibilities of being a good coach. A qualified coach is someone who will keep you honest about your own assessment, will listen and guide you, and will help you develop the strength and character you may be lacking. Someone who has been there, done that, and can offer possible perspectives without the emotional influences that can skew so many thoughts. Someone who doesn't see things the same way you do. Someone who can spot the blindside that may be fooling you into believing accolades that simply aren't true.

A coach knows his or her job is to not be you, to not sit in your seat, and to not buy into your story. Coaches train people by educating them and providing experiences to help them adopt new attitudes and actions, and then they offer regular honest feedback. They let others know when they are doing well and when they need to course correct.

I (Ed) was coaching Jessica towards her goal of adding a full twist to her back flip on floor. The simpler a move is to execute the more leeway the performer has to make mistakes. Foundational skills early on seem boring and redundant, and sometimes gymnasts become lax in their accuracy. They can still perform simple moves, even with a sloppy or bad technique, and they get fooled into thinking they have a good technique when they really don't. As the skill gets complicated, those weaknesses in foundational skills show up plain as day. Well, at least they do to the coach.

Jessica had fallen into a very bad habit of throwing her head back on a simple back flip in the laid out position (straight body with no tuck). Watch anybody on a trampoline, and you'll see this is probably the most common breach of foundational technique. The reason this body position absolutely won't work in a full twisting back flip is because when you throw your head back your body loosens up and arches. Arches don't like to twist. Straight lines or straight body positions twist more easily.

I told Jessica, "If you want to twist the lay out back, you have to keep your head forward."

"I am!" she responded adamantly.

"It may feel like that in the middle of the move, but from where my coach feet are standing, you're not even close," I said. That only aggravated her because in her mind I was telling her something she knew wasn't true.

She insisted, "I want you to spot me on a full twisting back flip."

"Jessica," I said, "if you throw your head back in the middle of a full twisting back flip, you will get halfway into the move, find out your body won't twist like you are imagining, crash and get hurt. You could even fall and hurt your neck." As a coach, I wanted Jessica to make the move, but not until she was willing to listen to my correction and make the move safely.

"Well, if you are afraid to spot me I will find somebody else," she huffed. I watched her as she pouted her way across the gym.

The next day, Jessica was willing to let me work with her again. I asked her to do some foundational skill exercises and as she flipped through the simple moves, I recorded her. When she hopped down off the mat, I showed the video to her.

"Jessica" I asked, "Now what do you see?"

"Wow, I am throwing my head back." She smiled at me, a little embarrassed.

Coaching and videos are reference points that reveal discrepancies between what a person thinks and the truth. A good coach always relates a problem, a leadership deficiency, or bad body position back to a foundational flaw and corrects from

Can anyone be a coach? We contend that anyone can coach who has:

- **Mutual respect with the person they are coaching.**
- **A desire to help and see people grow.**
- **Developed their personal coaching skills.**
- **Obtained coaching exercises, assessments, and training modules to use with their coachees.**

there the right way. From an outside reference point, the coach sees how habits, good and bad, can influence the outcome of the move.

The qualities needed to be a good coach are achievable. And the benefits are immeasurable. The most effective way to continue your personal growth as a leader is to coach others in their own leadership growth. Rather than assuming you are not good enough to coach someone else to be a better leader, or that coaching is not your leadership style, decide to take the impressive step of changing someone's life. As you exercise your personal leadership competencies throughout this book, you will gain the skills to coach others simply by becoming the kind of leader you are coaching others to be.

Motivating

So how can you leverage your influence to motivate others to action? There are three key motivational strategies that we see leaders use regularly—Fear, Incentive, and Purpose. Only one of these methods creates dynamic and lasting motivation.

Fear. Some leaders motivate by using force as a fear method. "Get this done by Friday or you will be working this weekend." This method only achieves a temporary result. Notice a speeding driver slow down when passing a highway patrol car, then resuming high speed once beyond the officer's sight. The driver slowed out of fear of receiving a ticket, but his motivation to abide by the speed limit vanished along with the looming threat. That is the way fear motivation works. It is temporary and due to an outside force pushing it. Once the force is no longer there, people resume their original bad behavior.

Externally driven force = Temporary fear motivation

Incentive. Other leaders motivate by using rewards, bonuses, and other incentive methods. The challenge with offering incentive as motivation is that it too will only get a temporary result. The consequence of this strategy is reflected in the saying: Today's incentives become tomorrow's expectations. If an incentive—bonus, day off, pizza party, promotion, etc.—is all that is used to influence and motivate people, then what will be done for them next time? Will management have to keep offering those rewards because that is all that seems to work and the employees now expect extra compensation with every task? In that case, what are the consequences if there is no next time?

We worked with an organization that brought us in to improve morale. Before we started our assignment, we met with the Executive Vice President of Administration and Finance who prepared us for the work that needed to be done. He said that ten months earlier the executive team had made a decision that turned out to negatively impact the company, resulting in the loss of many high-performing employees across the 700+ employee company. Morale and motivation were extremely low.

The Executive VP revealed the company had sustained three consecutive years of low to no profits. He shared that their decision came down to two choices. Either lay off approximately nine percent of the workforce, or cut the annual bonus program. After much consideration, they opted to cut the bonus program so that no one would be impacted by the trauma of being laid off.

Since we were brought in to turn morale around and get employees focused on a new strategy and direction, we reviewed their bonus program and what effect its termination might be having on their employees. We discovered that their bonus program had kept many employees still working for the company because it was based on longevity with the company, pay grade, and absenteeism. For many employees, it meant an additional fifteen to twenty percent of their salary.

So imagine you are a hardworking, high-producing employee who is extremely marketable and you just had twenty percent of your pay cut because your company is doing poorly. You may decide to leave also! The employees who remained were not necessarily the high-performing, tenured employees, so not only did we need to increase morale, we needed to improve productivity and get everyone in the company working towards a common vision, strategy, and goals.

We rolled out our Strategy Management for Teams program with all employees in multiple departments. We focused on 1) rebuilding trust, 2) improving communication and managing conflict, 3) corporate and departmental planning, 4) accountability and role responsibilities, and 5) focused execution for improved results. We created an operating plan that every department used to ensure that goals and projects were getting done. The result? A seventeen percent increase in revenues over two years, and eight percent profitability. So rather than use incentives to motivate employees as had been done in the past, we helped them attach to a purpose, which is a more effective, long-lasting type of motivation.

Externally driven bonuses and rewards = Temporary incentive motivation

Ultimately, an influential leader motivates others by helping them achieve a broader goal, a purpose and then showing them appreciation for their role in it.

Purpose. The most lasting way to motivate and influence others is through vision, feedback and training. People want to know what their purpose is and how that ties to the relationship or mission of the company. They want to know how you think they are doing in their job and what they need to do to improve if your answer is not outstanding. And people want you to invest in them and their development so they can continue to be of more value. And when they contribute, people want to be noticed for their accomplishments. By seeing how their projects and goals impact the organization's success, they know they matter.

Internally driven change = Permanent purposeful motivation

Most employees' motivational needs boil down to three basic things:
- Employees need **something to believe in** (the organization's vision, mission, purpose and direction).
- Employees need **someone to believe in** (a corporate or department leader(s) who leads effectively and makes good decisions).
- Employees need **someone to believe in them** (leaders who demonstrates trust and belief in their people, will give them opportunities for growth and advancement, and will compensate them fairly).

A workplace without these key attributes cultivates average performers. Average performers believe that if they apply more effort than the organization applies to itself, their effort is wasteful. So over time, people will reset their personal standard to the minimum of the organization. The best performers always apply themselves out of a moral obligation to themselves. Yet if this standard is higher than that of the organization or the team leader, it again feels wasteful. Typically, instead of resetting their standard to the bare minimum to get by, these high performers leave in search of a company that will value their work ethic. The result is a culture of mediocrity, driven by the people who stay and exist in tolerance. So it is critical for each leader to cultivate an atmosphere of motivation by helping employees see the bigger picture of the company and their purpose in it.

Understanding Appreciation

As we work with companies, we hear regularly the argument that employees get paid to do their job, so they should just do it without having to throw a party every time they accomplish something. But this blunt mentality ignores the primary need of all human beings to feel appreciated.

After years of training on how to motivate and engage employees in the workplace, we have learned that people have different ways they want to be appreciated. What might make one person feel valued isn't necessarily what will have the same effect on another.

Think of a time when you felt appreciated for something. The person appreciating you may have been a boss, a significant other, or a friend. What did that person say or do that really made you feel appreciated, loved, or respected? Was it a boss who gave you an extra day off of work? Was it a spouse who cooked and prepared your favorite meal? Was it a friend who called you personally to thank you for helping them out in time of need? Noticing what makes you feel valued and appreciated will help you understand the type of appreciation style you respond to best. And as a leader, you need to also become familiar with the appreciation preferences of others as well.

Leaders may be so closely aligned with their own personal motivations that the preferences of others elude them. Consequently, leaders tend to recognize or appreciate people in a fashion that is right for themselves. But their attempts at showing appreciation don't seem to land right because they are not offered in a way that is important to the recipient. So the leader doubles up on it, delivers it again, and then doubles up again until finally he decides the other person is just high maintenance. And even if this leader tries to apologize, he will most likely apologize with his own appreciation style, which of course will also fall flat.

Recognition repeated with the wrong style is actually a de-motivator and leads to frustration and bewilderment. Appreciation doesn't have to be delivered in truckload quantities to accomplish its purpose. It's all about delivery in a way the other person needs to receive it.

We were training and coaching at a large electronics distribution company that had about twenty managers in our one-year coaching program. One of the managers was said to have been voted Best Employee of the Year for the previous year, but since then, had gone AWOL. She and her team had lost visibility, they weren't going above and beyond to support other departments like before, etc.

In one of my coaching sessions with this manager, she mentioned that she had been humiliated when she received the award the previous year.

When I asked her what terrible thing had happened to cause her such humiliation, she said that she was asked to deliver a speech at the annual company luncheon on what it takes to be successful. This personal attention was not motivating for her at all, and in fact, had the opposite effect the award was supposed to have.

In our training, we teach *Seven Types of Appreciation Styles*. Developed before a number of similar love languages hit the self-help scene, our program helps leaders understand the importance of individual-specific appreciation. We show how people will only recognize that you love, value, and appreciate them if you convey that message in a way they can understand, and we put this all within the context of leadership.

The *Seven Types of Appreciation Styles* are:
1. **Trust**. Most people feel appreciated when you trust them, but some have a higher need for *trust* than others. Those who feel appreciated through *trust* are often (not always) people who

haven't always been treated with trust or respect in their past. So when you do trust them or show them respect, they feel the connection and kindness. Someone with a *trust* appreciation style will place great value in being trusted with confidential information or the responsibility of a special project at work. Giving this individual a gift may land as a nice gesture, but will not fulfill the appreciation need.

2. **Time.** Some people feel appreciation when you spend time with them. Not just in a group, but just with them. They take great value in the fact you are willing to give them your full attention.

> *During a coaching and training program I (Janet) was leading, I met with a manager who was one of the participants. I started the conversation by asking questions to help me understand his job.*
>
> *"What are your strengths as a manager?" I asked.*
>
> *He was struggling for an answer.*
>
> *So I probed. "If I were to ask your boss what your strengths are, what would he say?"*
>
> *His response surprised me. "I don't think my boss knows that I work for him."*
>
> *"Why do you say that?"*
>
> *"I have worked for him for two years. He has never been to one of my staff meetings, he has never asked me to lunch, and he has probably stopped by my office only twice."*
>
> *I wrote a note to myself that his appreciation style sounded like TIME.*
>
> *A week later I sat in his boss's office.*
>
> *I asked the boss, "What are John's strengths?"*
>
> *He quickly replied, "John is the best manager that I have ever had working for me."*
>
> *"Really?" I said.*
>
> *"John manages his people and time resources well," he continued, "and rallies his people around critical projects."*
>
> *I asked, "Do you think John knows that you value him this way?*
>
> *"Oh yeah."*

"How do you know?"

"I tell him all the time."

He then turned to his computer and pulled up an email that he had sent John two weeks prior to my meeting with John. In this email he was commending him and his team for an outstanding project delivery.

But there was a disconnect. John's appreciation style is "time." The boss was giving him "talk." John didn't recognize talk as appreciation. He just wanted time with his boss.

Time appreciation styles feel valued if you invite them to a baseball game, the movies, to your home for dinner, or out to lunch. They like to have meaningful conversations. A good way to recognize them is that they come into your office, sit down and start chatting about the weekend. They don't send you an email because their preferred communication is in person (*time*). So the worst thing you can do when they come into your office is to continue working on the computer, nodding at them to go ahead and talk because you are capable of multitasking. *Time* appreciation styles want you to stop what you are doing and give them your full attention. This applies to your spouse, children, coworkers, and friends who have this style.

3. **Talk**. People who have *talk* as their appreciation style are people who like to hear the words describing what they did well, how they are loved, and what others admire most about them. People who have this style feel energized, loved, valued, and appreciated when they are told "You look great in that outfit," or "I really got a lot out of your training session," or "What you did the other day for me made me feel special." These words melt their heart and inspire more effort. Positive talk motivates people to do more for the person who is saying it, because they want to hear more. Someone's gift of words is more valuable to this type of person than buying them a gift (*token*) or asking them to dinner (*time*).

   The challenge with this appreciation style is that some of those with other appreciation styles (especially *take action* styles) think talk is cheap, and that anyone can say the right words. This is not a belief that the *talk* appreciation style holds. *Talk* appreciation styles believe the positive feedback is sincere when they hear it. If *talk* appreciators don't receive adequate positive feedback, they may resort to asking for it or bragging in hopes somebody else will continue the conversation. They ask, "What did you think of my presentation?" or "What did you think of the dinner that I cooked?" In their questions, they are longing to know they are indeed appreciated.

If *talk* is your appreciation style then it is important to understand how your need to hear affirmative talk may be perceived. If a person with another style hears you asking for verbal recognition, they may think you are needy or full of yourself, and wonder why should I give that boastful person any recognition? It looks like they give plenty of it to themselves.

This shows the importance of understanding the appreciation styles of others as well as our own, so neither party gets left out of feeling loved, valued or appreciated.

4. **Tokens**. This is the most expensive way to appreciate people or influence behavior. People with the *token* appreciation style feel appreciated when you buy or give them things. To these *token* style individuals a token of appreciation says that you care. It relays the message that you took the time to pick something out just for them. They like to receive something tangible that you have taken the time to shop for and have spent your money on. It may be flowers, candy, a new car, a bottle of wine, or even money itself. Anything great or small. As an example of the difference between a *token* style and a *time* style, the *time* style wants you to invite them to lunch, while the *token* style would prefer you give them the gift card to the restaurant.

    As a reminder, *token* styles tend to give tokens because they relate to that sense of appreciation.

5. **Take Action**. These people feel appreciated when you do something for them. Actions like handling a customer crisis on their day off or covering their shift in a pinch. This kind of action legitimizes the value of a *take action* appreciation style, and expands their environment, whether home or business,

into a sense of belonging.

> *I (Janet) had an assistant who told me one day about the struggles she was having with her landlord. She mentioned that he doesn't fix things when they break and that he was a nasty person to talk with. A few weeks later, an article came out in the newspaper about what to do with a bad landlord. Already knowing that she had a take action style, I read the article, cut it out of the newspaper and brought it into work. In her next performance appraisal, she told me how much that meant to her. That was easy!*

Something to take note of, however, is to make sure you take action in a way that the *take action* recipient likes. If you clean the desk for your assistant or your boss, for example, make sure you put things back in the place where she likes them kept.

6. **Tell Others.** This is *talk* appreciation style on steroids. People with the appreciation style of *tell others* like the positive feedback to be delivered in front of others so that multiple people can notice their accomplishment. They appreciate awards and trophies, especially if they are displayed in a public viewing area.

   They also feel special when they receive the feedback from a third party. For example, if I tell a coworker how much I like the way my trainer delivered the last training session, and my coworker happens to mention to the trainer that "Janet said she really liked the way you delivered your training session last Thursday," the *tell others* appreciation style trainer will glow with pride.

7. **Touch.** We left the trickiest for last. *Touch* styles feel valued through hugs, handshakes, a quick touch to the shoulder, etc. They desire appreciation through affection. Assume you have a friend who greets you every time with a hug, and if *touch* is not your appreciation style, it might make you uncomfortable. So you respond by holding back a little and diverting the hug into a light tap. The message the hugger receives is that you are uncomfortable with him (not the hug). So he doesn't feel appreciated, loved, valued, and so on.

In many workplaces, the only acceptable touch is a handshake. It is easy to identify people who want appreciation and acceptance through *touch* because when you reach out to shake their hand, they grab on to your elbow and often hang on while delivering a greeting. They might stand closer to you than most, or even go in for the irresistible hug.

You might find that you like two or three of these appreciation styles. Keep in mind that appreciation styles can sometimes shift based on what is currently lacking in your life. For example, let's say the two appreciation styles that you like most are *trust* and *time*, and although you occasionally go to lunch with a few people in the office, you don't feel trusted in your personal or professional life. The people you interact with daily don't seem to understand you or value you. Therefore, they don't come to you with questions, they don't ask you for your opinion, and they don't give you any meaningful projects. As a result of feeling unappreciated you change jobs, where you quickly gain the trust of your coworkers and management. You are given meaningful projects and responsibilities, and you feel appreciated. Now let's say in this new company, that although your boss and coworkers trust you by handing off projects, they rarely spend any time with you. No one on the team asks you to lunch or stops by your office to chat. So the primary appreciation style that is now missing in your life is *time*, whereas before it was *trust*. This change in style tends to occur when one specific need remains severely neglected for a length of time. If appreciation is presented at the right time, the right way, it doesn't take much appreciation to go a long way with someone.

It is important to take the time to recognize the appreciation styles of the people who are most important to you, and that includes coworkers, especially direct reports. One indicator is how

If you're having difficulty trying to determine the appreciation style of others, just ask. Say "Think of a time when someone showed that they cared or appreciated you. What did they say or do?" Then listen in their answer for an appreciation style.

they appreciate others. It is common to naturally appreciate others the way that we want to be appreciated, so observe the methods others choose.

Expressing appreciation to people in their preferred styles can alter their behavior, establish expectations, and energize gratitude to the exciting core. Most certainly, a leader who learns how to effectively show appreciation to others will have tremendous influence in their lives. And when a leader shows enthusiasm, her influence increases all the more.

Enthusiasm

One of the most productive leadership qualities we've seen that can motivate a team to greater performance is the leader's level of enthusiasm. Enthusiasm by many is perceived as childish, bubbly, and not professional. However, the right level of enthusiasm at the right time can have a very positive impact on a team's performance.

Observe the difference between these two mindsets of two company managers who just got a huge order from one of their customers. They are meeting with their staff to alert them they are going to have to work hard to fill the order:

1. "We just landed the biggest deal in the history of our company, thanks to John! This deserves a celebration. I encourage everyone to take off a couple of hours early for the weekend to energize yourselves, because come Monday, this order is going to have us working our tails off to create a happy customer. And that's what we do around here....create happy, satisfied customers, thanks to all of you. Have a wonderful weekend!"

2. "As we all know, when we get a big order like the one that came in today, we have to work harder than normal. I don't want to hear complaints about working overtime next week because that is what you signed up for when you took the job. After all, you will get your overtime pay."

The difference between these managers is... enthusiasm! Enthusiasm can make an average place to work, great! An enthusiastic leader, employee, or coworker demonstrates that he wants to be in the present moment and will give all that he has to get the job done. Have you ever heard the saying that people don't leave companies, they leave bosses? Who wants to work or be in a relationship with someone who is emotionally dull, negative, or depressing? Can you imagine the discouragement of playing on a basketball team with a coach who never smiles or gets excited about the game? The best part about being enthusiastic is that it is within your control. Maybe you haven't been the best boss, but no one understands your department better than you do and what it takes to deliver a service to your internal or external customer. So rather than dwell on what you haven't done right, focus on practicing some of the exercises in this book. You can choose to adopt an enthusiastic mindset and watch others brighten around you as a result.

Enthusiasm sells! It contributes to how influential you are. There are many ways to demonstrate enthusiasm. Consider the following:

- In a job interview, do you sit up straight, smile a lot, make eye contact and discuss the positive experiences or training your previous employer gave you?
- As an employee, do you show up on time, volunteer for projects, demonstrate a willingness to ask questions and listen, and show interest in your job?
- As a boss, do you regularly meet one-on-one with your people for purposes of development and support rather than only checking in on them around metrics or their job tasks?
- As a spouse, do you make vacation, restaurant, and date night suggestions and offer to help out when your loved one is overloaded?
- As a parent, do you encourage your children to try out for the team, listen to their ideas, dreams, and even failures, as well as support them while they're doing their homework?
- As a friend, do you call to stay in touch, acknowledge birthdays, invite friends over for dinner, and be there for them when they are going through a life crisis?

Overall, a person with enthusiasm comes across as wanting to make someone else's day better. In doing so, the collective organization, team or family is better.

So how do you cultivate a mindset of enthusiasm? Think about your assets. What is going well for you? The more time you spend focusing on the things you do well in life, the less time you will have to dwell on the negative. By paying less attention to the negatives, it's likely that they will diminish or even vanish on their own.

Consider this simple exercise of finishing the following seven sentences every night (or once a week) before going to bed:

- I am thankful for....
- My most significant accomplishment for today is....
- Other people compliment me on my ability to....
- I feel really good about myself when....
- I am proud of my ability to....
- Something I would like other people to know about me is....
- Something nice I did for someone else was....

Negative Informal Leaders

There are people who tend to have a negative influence on others, at times even destructive. These are most often informal leaders with no management title, but who are naturally wired and have an appetite for leadership nonetheless. They have such a high need to lead that they will oppose current leadership by leading others in the opposite direction. They would rather lead negatively than not lead at all.

These negative informal leaders lack integrity, an attitude of accountability, or leadership skills, so they end up negatively influencing others in an effort to be heard or noticed. This can look like bad-mouthing the company, their manager, or coworkers. It may look like a person who employs terror or terrorism as a political weapon. The negative informal leader leads others into their erroneous way of thinking, which is counterproductive to the goals of a department, company, state, or country.

Managers who are able to identify their informal leaders (those wired for leadership but with no official leadership role) have the opportunity to steer their direction of influence. When a manager builds positive relationships with informal leaders, keeps lines of communication open, and gives them opportunities for project or people leadership, the manager is exercising a positive influence. As a result, not only is this manager leading with influence but she is also freeing herself from some of her formal management responsibility. Because she has cultivated positive informal leaders to influence and lead others, the managing leader has opened up more time to do the things that are most valuable to the success of the organization.

Know your employees' appreciation styles, and offer regular feedback to let them know how they are doing. Feedback develops and nurtures an individual's purpose. This interaction inspires people to want to work harder if they know that someone else cares about them as a person and their development. Employees are motivated to dedicate themselves to a company if they feel valued and appreciated for the work that they do, are communicated with and feel they are included, and know that what they do matters to something or someone else that is bigger or even more important than themselves.

This demonstration of leadership is not only for the workplace. It is for the home, and in your community as well. Think back for a moment on someone who has had the most influence on you personally or professionally. Was it a parent, a teacher, a coach, a boss? Observe how you quickly move past this person's title, and on to the deeper influence this person conveyed. What did they do or say that influenced you the most? Did they seem to understand what makes you tick and develop your sense of purpose on the team or in the world? Did they demonstrate a personal enthusiasm for helping you grow and change? Did they help you reach your goals?

Influential leaders who genuinely are interested in helping other people grow in their knowledge, their projects, their behavior, and their attitude are people who others will look back on with gratitude and say, "You really made a difference in my life."

I (Janet) was on an airplane when a gentleman in his 70s sat down in the seat next to me. He asked me where I was traveling to and then proceeded to tell me that he was flying to Florida to connect with a long-time friend and business associate who had mentored him through his 30s and 40s. He said that his mentor friend was about ten years older than he was and so he wanted to specifically fly down to Ft. Lauderdale before it was too late to let his friend know what a positive impact he had made on his life and career. He shared that his mentor friend was always willing to listen to his successes, ideas, and complaints. He described his mentor friend as a man of integrity who would always speak the truth whether you wanted to hear it or not. Then the gentleman became very excited when he told me that his friend didn't even know that he was coming. His visit was going to be a surprise, and appreciating his friend was the sole purpose for his travel to Florida.

It made me wonder if I could ever be that person of influence who would cause someone else to want to appreciate me in that way. Years ago, I read a book by Dr. Phil McGraw and he talked about being a positive, pivotal person. I made a decision that day that I would try to be a positive, pivotal person to at least ten people per year. Since then, ten has been my baseline performance, and one hundred is the goal.

I hope that someday someone will call or fly to see me to tell me that my influence made a positive difference in his or her life. That would be the ultimate confirmation of a job well done.

ADVICE FROM YOUR COACH

Decide that you will be a positive, pivotal person in some-one's life every day. Appreciate them, teach them something meaningful, listen to their ideas, and give them purpose. You will leave this world a better place for doing so.

LEADERSHIP EXERCISES
INFLUENCE

Leadership Exercise #9: GIVING POSITIVE FEEDBACK

Exercise Purpose: To influence others through positive feedback reminders.

Expected Outcome: To practice giving verbal appreciation by using the three-step positive feedback formula listed below, which in turn will get you into the habit of demonstrating enthusiasm and appreciation for the people who matter to you.

Positive feedback motivates people. It has an energy to it, both in the giving and in the receiving. However, positive feedback is only positive when meant with authenticity, and most effective when given individually as opposed to an entire team.

- Start every day with five coins in your right pocket. Focus on handing out praise and/or appreciation to at least five people every day. Every time you give a person positive feedback, move a coin to the other pocket. Continue this as a reminder until all five coins are transferred to the other pocket. This will get you into the habit of experiencing the joy when you give positive feedback to others.

- When verbally appreciating people, use the following three step formula:

    1. **Tell the person *what* you like**. *("Thank you so much for staying late last night to work on this report.")*

    2. **Tell the person *why* you like it**. *("I really appreciate this extra effort because now we will be well prepared as a department to handle any questions or issues that arise in the meeting today.")*

    3. **Ask the person a question about what you appreciate**. *("How did you know that John wanted to specifically see the conclusions from your client meeting?")*

Leadership Exercise #10: THE SEVEN APPRECIATION STYLES EXERCISE

Exercise Purpose: To identify individual appreciation styles that will most effectively motivate a person with a result of a more natural and genuine improvement in performance.

Expected Outcome: To appreciate people in a way that they can recognize by identifying specific ways to appreciate individual people or types of people.

Exercise Example:
Identify the ten most important people (those especially whom you want to positively influence) in your personal and professional life. Here are a few examples to get you started.

Employee, Family Member, Or Friend	Appreciation Style	Action That You Will Take
Example: Sally	Tell Others	Give her an opportunity to present the departmental plan to senior management.
Example: John	Trust	Give him an opportunity to occasionally work from home.
Example: Polly	Tokens/Talk	Buy her a salt and pepper shaker for her collection and include a note of appreciation.
Example: Sam	Time/ Take Action	Ask Sam and his family over for a barbeque as well as give him the opportunity to leave work early to take night classes at the community college.

Make it a point to do something that meets their appreciation style every week. Here are some appreciation ideas that you may want to use if you are having difficulty thinking of some.

Talk:

1. Praise, with specific positive feedback.
2. Write a letter of appreciation or recommendation.
3. Say "Thank you."

Take Action:

1. Let someone go home early from work, or let her work from home.
2. Do something for someone that is normally his job to do.
3. Train or provide training to someone in an area of importance to him.

Tokens:

1. Give someone a gift card to a favorite store or restaurant.
2. Buy a gift or tickets to a concert or game.
3. Provide a more desirable office, workspace, or more comfortable chair.

Time:

1. Take them to lunch or dinner.
2. Listen to their challenge or idea.
3. Hold regular staff meetings.

Tell Others:

1. Verbally appreciate them in front of others.
2. Award or give someone a certificate of accomplishment.
3. Start a staff meeting by letting people share their accomplishments.

Trust:

1. Seek their opinions and suggestions more often.
2. Reveal something of yourself by talking about your problems or experiences.
3. Delegate a project that has been your "baby."

Touch:
1. Shake someone's hand (or fist bump) to thank him or greet him.
2. If someone stands close to you, don't back up.
3. Give someone a big ole bear hug.

On the next page, write down specific people whom you would like to positively influence in your life. Think of direct reports, coworkers, family members, and friends. If you can't identify their appreciation style, go and ask them. Say "What is something that someone has said or done to really make you feel appreciated?" Then see if that idea reveals their appreciation style. Also, remember that people can have more than one appreciation style. They may be so deficient of appreciation that any and all of what you do will be helpful.

APPRECIATION STYLES CHART

Employee, Family Member, Or Friend	Appreciation Style	Action That You Will Take

A Goal

While lost in a gaze on I-25
Just thinking of all that could be,
I questioned the need for this everyday drive
For everyone that I could see.

Their faces don't change much one day to the next,
Their goal is to just get ahead,
This feeling had left me a little perplexed
To factors I'm facing ahead.

I thought for a minute of people I've known
Who seemed to have life well in hand,
Aside from the virtues and wisdom has grown
A common unanimous strand.

A dream and a goal are different events
On opposite ends of the earth,
One floats in the air with no consequence
The other has definite worth.

The first step converting a dream to a goal
They said is avoiding delay,
Along with the riches and peace in their soul
Their goal was to write one today.

By Ed Beard, Copyright 2015

Competency Seven
FUTURE FOCUS

In this Chapter, we will:

- Teach you the seven-step process for setting goals, including an example and worksheet to follow.

- Recognize the mindset for setting goals.

- Learn how to assess "where you stand now" in relation to "where you want to go."

- Develop a personal plan for leadership success.

Chapter Seven
FUTURE FOCUS

*In the absence of clearly defined goals, we are forced to focus
on activity and ultimately become enslaved to it.*

Up and down the front range of the Colorado Rocky Mountains, adventure seekers of all ages are scouring the hillsides in search of secret treasure. Well, to be precise, they are looking for strategically hidden containers, called geocaches. Geocaching is a high-tech, real-world, outdoor treasure hunting game. Participants download the coordinates where a treasure is hidden, and then they navigate to the hiding spot, following their charted course with the guidance of their GPS-enabled devices. Once the geocache is located, the successful hunter gets to share the details of his search with the online community of fellow geocachers. It's a growing sport with enthusiastic popularity for good reasons. Who doesn't love the intrigue of searching for hidden treasure?

Geocachers dream of discovering unique surprises buried within the secretly hidden caches. They also envision the satisfaction they'll feel after following challenging routes and twisting paths, and at long last they discover the secret hiding place and the joy of sharing the adventure with other geocache enthusiasts.

Now imagine a geocache team without a GPS. They may very well have the finest mountain climbers and outdoor gear, yet without a GPS to chart their course and guide them to the hidden treasure, they would wander in the woods aimlessly, and may even get lost in the expansive wilderness. Let's back up even further. What if a group of eager geocachers keep talking about setting up a search, but no one makes a plan. They all agree it's a great idea and talk about going sometime. Unless a leader takes charge to schedule a date, download the coordinates, gas up the car and pack the picnic lunch, the trip doesn't happen.

The geocache community sets a good example for the rest of us.

They have the motivation of a dream to discover treasure, a GPS to guide them, and a plan to accomplish their mission. We see this commitment as the ideal pattern for living life with a *future focus*.

Future focused means being intentional about what is ahead of you. When you are focused on your future instead of getting bogged down in everyday life, you are dreaming of what you want, setting goals as a declaration to pursue it, and devising a plan to achieve it.

Let's take a closer look at each of these three essential steps of living with a purposeful future focus: Dream, Goal, and Plan.

Dream

The power of visualization and imagining yourself being, doing, or having something is a powerful pull. It is why we have to be purposeful, even protective, of what we fill our minds with as well as visualize. Your dreams represent your vision for the future. Imagine that time, money, and resources were no obstacle. What new opportunities would now be worth pursuing?

I (Janet) decided back in 2000 that it would be fun and motivating to get our sales team together to understand each other's personal dreams, goals, and motivators by creating Dream/Vision boards. We closed the office one afternoon, brought in wine, cheese and hors d'oeuvres, plenty of magazines with pictures, and gave everyone a 20" x 30" foam poster board.

First, we each made a list of our dreams. We approached our dreams from the perspective of: "If time, money, and effort were no obstacle, I would like to be, have, or do…" After we each had written our dreams, we shared some of our dreams with each other. We then looked through magazines for pictures to support one another's dreams that we would use to make a collage of our dream pictures on our poster boards.

One of my financial dreams that I mentioned to the team was to be able to buy myself the new Jaguar S-Type 4.0 that had just come on the market. I loved the looks of the beautiful car with a round grill in the front, and I wanted mine in British racing green. As one of my team members was leafing through magazines, she found a picture of the exact car I wanted, not in the green that I wanted, but in blue. So up it went on my dream board that sits in my office still to this day.

Two years later, I decided to start looking for a new car, as my lease was a couple of months away from expiring on my current vehicle. After dreaming of Jaguar S-Type for two years, I decided I was finally able to go for it. I called the dealership and they told me that they did not have the color I wanted nor did any other dealer on the West Coast. They suggested that I come down to the dealership to look at the many different colors that were available. I decided on the way that if I needed to settle for black, red, or white, that I would consider those colors as well.

When I walked onto the lot of the Jaguar dealer, there was a beautiful blue Jaguar S-type 4.0 up on the car rack proudly standing above the rest. When I saw it, I knew this was my car! So I bought it and drove it home a few hours later.

The next morning, I woke up super excited to drive my new Jaguar. When I went outside and took a look at it again, I wondered what had possessed me to buy a blue car. This color may have been last on my list when I considered the possibilities on my way to the dealership.

That morning I drove my car to work, walked into my office, and realized that what had been staring back at me for the last two years was the exact blue color Jaguar from my dream board.

Dreaming is a powerful motivator of goals. Without taking time to dream, your goals may be fewer and far between. How do you decide what goals to set and develop a plan to achieve them?

A successfully accomplished plan is an outcome of a vision for the future. And part of this vision comes from taking the time to dream about what could be.

In the chart below, you will notice that all dreams (goals without target dates), start with courageous confidence and belief that you can accomplish what you set out to do as discussed in the first chapter. But having the confidence and dreams aren't enough. You also need a reason or motivation for wanting the goal. When all three of these factors come together, then a goal can be set.

Goal

Goal

Imagine that the game of soccer has no goals, no goalies, and no goal posts with nets. The soccer coach says to his players, "Go out on the field and run around for forty-five minutes, then we will take a break, and then you can run around for another forty-five minutes." There are no ways to score points because there are no goals. There is no satisfaction in this game, other than the exercise of running around. Would this look like the most popular sport in the world anymore? The athletes need a goal to kick the ball into and a purpose for taking action. And so it is with leaders. The actions that we take are motivated by plans, plans are motivated by goals, and goals are motivated by lofty dreams. We may not all aspire to win the World Cup, but whatever our dreams, we need clear goals to reach them.

The classic definition of a goal is a dream with a plan and a deadline. We each need goals to guide us. Setting goals is like mapping out your course to a desired destination. Goal setting is in reality the establishment of a relationship between where you are now and where you are going. A goal provides a sense of direction and keeps us focused on what is important so we don't veer off course. Goals serve as criteria for making daily choices and decisions, and to reflect back on to measure progress or identify the cause for a variance from the projected end point.

Goal clarity (i.e. writing, mapping, charting the way) allows energy to be directed toward attaining the goal because you know where you want to go, and what distractions to avoid. As a result, less time and energy are wasted in pursuing activities that are not goal-related.

Our experience suggests that there are two critical derailers that can prevent individuals from achieving their goals. They are: unforeseen obstacles and unrealistic time frames. Visualizing the end of the goal is what motivates you towards working on the right things and going in the right direction every day.

> *Marco joined us for a leadership development program recently, and in an effort to get to know people better, we found ourselves in a discussion around personal interests. It's insightful and just plain fun to know the kinds of things people are interested in and what they like to spend their time doing. Marco's personal passion is to ride motorcycles really, really fast. Not just one hundred miles per hour kind of fast but more like two hundred and fifty miles per hour fast. That is a whole other kind of fast.*
>
> *At two hundred and fifty miles per hour, Marco shared that you don't really have good contact with the pavement. It's like you're floating but not really. The rules of control change at high speeds and the motorcycle is steered by shifting your weight from side to side, and although the contact with the pavement seems disconnected, it's all that there is to use. Marco also shared something else that is worth passing along. He was asked how he processes fast enough at this speed to make the turns, avoid obstacles, and think about what has to happen. What was so insightful was when Marco said, "The faster you go, the further down the road you have to be focused."*

This scenario plays out so frequently with the leadership development culture of a business, especially within an ambitious, fast-growing company. The pace is swift and the to do list like yeast seems to propagate itself. Every day brings with it an urgency that needs attention, and these urgent demands can distract a leader's focus, while the business is still advancing at two hundred and fifty miles per hour. Then the future is met with a string of disasters because they weren't noticed ahead of time—employees are not in the right role, or the management skills of the leader are not prepared for the upcoming changes, or those "trust and accountability" issues with a particular manager that revealed themselves long ago now blow up and cause more damage than had they been dealt with in a timely manner. Leadership had not been looking far enough ahead, but rather at the task right in front of them. By the time the hazard is seen and it registers as a problem, the collision is inevitable, the business goes into an uncontrollable wobble and crashes, and now the leader is consumed with damage control. The problems that were viewed as eventually needing attention arrived with great force, and now the universe has taken over and set the rules and outcome of the crash.

Surprise obstacles can rob a person of energy and add hopelessness because the goal seems to get more difficult. The ability to look down the road helps a leader determine what priorities to set, what potential problems to avert and what solutions to implement for those problems that can't be avoided. This kind of future focus leads to personal success and ultimately leadership and business success.

Throughout life people set goals, although sometimes on a sub-conscious level. People will often avoid writing goals with the excuse "I don't need to write anything. I can keep my important goals in my head." But just *having* a goal is not enough. Staying on course requires writing goals down, organizing them, and prioritizing them.

Some individuals may perceive goal setting as holistic nonsense. In their mind they are so intimately connected to what they want (call it a goal or not) that there is no real need to write it down. It's interesting how long they will let their goal orbit their mind and not realize it's still orbiting like it was last year. Absolutely, goals can be achieved without taking a written step, however the success rate for achievement is proven to be higher if goals are put to paper. So if a key to success is to reach your goals, then do what it takes to reach them. Write them down.

There is something in the act of writing a goal down that makes it real, gives it permanence. Unwritten goals cannot be read and reviewed, and therefore are easily forgotten or changed. Written goals that are reviewed regularly become reality. Also, unless the goal is written, there is little effort spent on realizing the potential obstacles ahead of time.

Writing goals also connects a person's mind to the realistic time needed to achieve the goal right from the start. As progress towards achieving the goal plays out over time, it doesn't lose energy because the realistic time frame was planned up front.

Studies conclude time after time that written goals, along with a plan for action to attain them, are the most frequently accomplished. Although heralded as a myth, a well-known study shared by Mark McCormack ("What They Don't Teach You in the Harvard Business School") and Brian Tracey (*Goals!*) reveals some startling information about the importance of written goals. Only 3% of the people interviewed had any definite, written plans for achievement. Another 10% had a fairly good notion of their aims and objectives. 60% had given a little thought to it, but mainly in the financial area. The balance, or 27% had never given any serious thought to goal setting or planning for the future. It is no surprise that, among these people, only 3% were highly successful, 10% were moderately well-off, 60% were people of modest means, and the remainder were just barely getting by with the help of government support or family charity.

The most interesting part of the survey revealed that the second group, the 10%, had the same qualifications as the top 3%, equal education, talent and intelligence. They were ambitious and knew where they were going. The only measurable difference between the two groups lay in the fact that the top 3% had committed to write their goals.

Leaders are business people, and one of the differences that separates the successful from the mediocre is that the successful leaders are those with a written business plan, especially when the leader includes his team in the goal setting and business plan development.

In a meeting with a CEO and business owner, he remarked that he was sick and tired of his leaders not reaching goals. He expanded this by saying that for the last five consecutive years, they had not reached their revenue goals nor experienced any profit as an organization. And he was frustrated.

I (Janet) asked, "Do you give them the revenue, profit, and performance goals, or do you get them involved in the process?" I concluded from his answer that he did NOT get them involved in the process, which is part of the reason why there was no buy-in for accomplishing the goals.

So we gathered his eighteen executive and departmental leaders together for a two-day planning session. The vision, mission, values, and long-range goals were already clearly defined, so we focused on developing the annual goals. We discussed what was going right, what was going wrong, what was missing, and what was confusing in the organization, in their branches, in their departments, with their customers, and in the industry. The result of the process netted seven clearly defined annual organizational goals. Now all eighteen leaders had their marching orders. They were each given three weeks to have their seven departmental goals clearly defined (one annual, four quarterly, and two semi-annual) after meeting with each of their respective teams.

Three weeks later we met again with the leaders. They all presented their goals, listing obstacles and discussing how they were going to solve them. They showed us their action items with target dates, budget requirements, staff needed, etc. Then I took all of these 128 goals, and 792 action items (small goals) and created an operating plan that they put on their company's shared system for all to access and update weekly.

Every month, this team met, but only to discuss the progress on the goals and challenges meeting them. At the end of the year, this organization experienced an increase in revenue with 16% profits.

Just as we may individually set goals, a company must start with a vision (dreams), set goals, and have an operating plan to accomplish them. And no one single person in the organization should do this alone. It takes everyone being fully vested in setting goals, which leads to organizational success.

(At the end of this chapter we have provided a goal/project planning process form for you to follow when writing out your goals. You can also go to our website **www.TheEmployersEdge.com** for a free download of this form.)

Following are ideas to help you accomplish your written goals:

1. **State goals in specific and measurable terms**. Ask yourself, "How will I know when I've achieved this goal?" Even intangible goals need tangible indicators. If you have a goal to be more patient, count how many times you raise your voice in

a month. If the number drops, your patience is increasing. Some examples of goal statements generated by past clients include:

    a.   Increase revenue (sales) by 10% over last year's sales.

    b.   Develop and monitor procedures for quality assurance personnel domestically and internationally.

    c.   Bring in sufficient inventory to meet the sales demand based on the purchasing forecast.

    d.   Increase ticket volume to 25%.

    e.   Identify decision-making authorities for each member of the executive team by the end of the month.

    f.   Develop an 8-hour team-training program that builds team skills of trust, communication, and accountability.

    g.   Decrease shipping errors from 2% to 1%.

    h.   Write job descriptions for all employees by xx/xx/xxxx.

2. **Identify the benefits of achievement.** Know the rewards and dreams that personally motivate you to achieve the goal. Ask yourself, "What's my reward? Why do I want to accomplish this goal?" List every possible reward or benefit you will enjoy when you've achieved your goal. If you can't think of any specific reasons for doing something, you won't! And perhaps you shouldn't.

3. **Identify the consequences associated with not achieving the goal.** If you know that missing a goal or project deadline could mean losing the government contract that results in laying off multiple employees, this can help motivate accurate planning and goal attainment.

    Why write down these motivators, both benefits and consequences? Because goals can be difficult to accomplish when we lose sight of why they are so important. When you have written reminders as to why the goal is important, it becomes the nitrogen boost needed to catapult you forward.

4. **Set goals that are realistic.** We encourage you to dream big, and then set realistic goals to achieve them. If you have never earned over $60,000 a year and you've established that as your

average for a long time, don't suddenly decide overnight your earning level will jump to $100,000, unless you have a new plan with realistic and achievable steps. Many people are not capable of making the personality and the work habit changes necessary to have such a sudden increase in earning ability. But if you set realistic goals and work on them, you can get big results. Remember, Janet didn't earn her Jaguar overnight.

Genuine goal setting is the first step toward positive, overt action. The next step is putting together a plan of how to accomplish those goals.

Plan

Consider these essential elements of putting together a plan to accomplish your goals:

1. **Plan action steps for achieving your goals.** Break goals into small, manageable segments that you can accomplish one at a time. Ask yourself, "What do I have to do to accomplish my goal?" The specific activities become your action steps to goal attainment. Then, plan every day's activities by taking an action step that will get you closer to your goals.

2. **Set target dates and deadlines for achieving your goals.** Set target dates and deadlines for each step. Having deadlines looming will cause you to keep pressing on. Deadlines are the foundation of commitment. When you are committed to accomplish an action by a certain date, you will be boosted by the adrenaline to keep that commitment. You may even discover new ways of doing things as you figure out how to finish on time. Deadlines are the instigators of achievement and inventiveness. A goal without a deadline is merely a philosophical statement.

3. **Identify the sacrifices and/or trade-offs you will need to make to accomplish the goal.** So often, we set goals without giving attention to the amount of time that it will take to reach it. Most people do not find an extra thirty hours in any given month to accomplish a new goal. Therefore, thought must be given to what you are willing to sacrifice or give up. If you are in a management position, this may look like delegating some of the action items in order to get to the goal. Or

it may look like delegating another responsibility to a willing coworker in order for you to focus on the new goal.

The reality is, people are more apt to place trust, commitment, and energy in leaders who have a plan, a direction. If you as a leader don't shape your goals and plans in writing, don't be surprised if your team is lethargic about following your lead. If you do have a plan, your team will appreciate that you've already anticipated the obstacles and have a strategy that has a high chance of success. And remember, plans sometimes morph and develop as new situations arise, or as you discover new significant information. Just know that dreams and goals can only be achieved when you adopt a plan to get them.

Every October, the Denver Botanical Gardens creates a human-sized maze carved into several cornfields. You can wind your way through acres of seven-foot-tall corn stalks, and even view the design from two fifteen-foot-tall illuminated bridges that overlook the giant corn maze. With advanced planning, people can download and print an aerial view map of the corn maze from their website to help them navigate through the maze a little faster. Without the map, it can take visitors anywhere from one to three hours to get from start to finish.

The first year that our family (Janet) went to the corn maze, we had no idea how difficult it would be and how lost we would get. We kept running into the same people over and over who were also looking for the right path that would eventually lead them to the exit. We had been in the corn maze for a little over an hour, when I happened to notice a slip of paper in between a few corn stalks along the path. Because it was noticeably out of place and looked like litter, I stooped down to pick it up. It was a map of the corn maze.

I told my family that I found a map of the maze, and another family nearby heard me. So we started to follow the map, and the other family naturally started to follow us. Soon, others who were lost in the corn maze learned that our path through the maze was based on a map. By the time that we exited the maze, we had about twenty to thirty people follow us right out of the maze.

The point is this: If you have a direction, and others know that you have a map, game plan, business plan, departmental plan, or whatever you want to call it, others will sense enough trust in your plan, and will follow. This is leadership!

Leadership success doesn't just happen. It is the result of conscious, deliberate effort identified through goal setting and planning, followed by actions, that convert those goals into reality. The power of being a future-focused leader comes from clearly defined goals, having a definite personalized plan of action and working every day on that plan.

ADVICE FROM
YOUR COACH

Focus on the future and challenge yourself to put your goals in writing. Start by creating a "dream list" for your personal and professional life. Then create goals for all areas of your life. From there put your plan in writing. A written plan will help you crystallize your thoughts and motivate you to action.

LEADERSHIP EXERCISES
FUTURE FOCUS

Leadership Exercise #11: GOAL PLANNING PROCESS

Exercise Purpose: To identify the parameters of your goal, put it in writing, and identify with clarity the first step necessary to act on it.

Expected Outcome: To have a completed goal or project planning guide to help ensure that you accomplish your goal.

(For a free download of the Goal/Project Planning worksheet on the next page, please feel free to visit our website at **www. TheEmployersEdge.com**)

On the next page, you will see a sample goal sheet filled out. Let's imagine that you own a small company. You know that the key to success is to grow sales by hiring a sales person. The SMART goal stated on the next page is to "Hire and train a new sales person to generate 8 new clients by 11/1." Take a look at the Goal Sheet and see how the thinking process unfolds.

GOAL/PROJECT PLANNING WORKSHEET

Today's Date: January 1st	Target Date: October 1st	Actual Completion Date:
Estimated Time to Complete: 73.5 hours	**Estimated Cost:** $300 plus my time/salary	**Personal:** _____ **Business:** _____

Goal/Project *(What do you want to accomplish?)*

Hire and fully train a new sales person to generate 8 new clients by 11/1

Benefits *(Why do you want it?)* Grow the company Less time prospecting and more time training	**Consequences** *(What could you lose?)* Not meet revenue goals
Obstacles *(What's keeping you from reaching this goal?)*	**Solutions** *(How will you overcome the obstacles?)*
1. Time to recruit and train	1. Block off two days up front, and two hours once a week dedicated to product, industry, or sales training
2. So much product training for a sales rep to learn at once	2. Focus on training sales person in the four most profitable products/ programs that we offer.
3. Finding an experienced quality applicant that fits my corporate culture	3. Put together a job description, competencies, interview questions, and check references and give an assessment to identify the best fit.
4. No recruitment budget	4. Send out email to my contacts with the job description attached to see if they can refer someone.
5.	5.

Resource List *(What do you need to accomplish it? Money, Time, People, Things?)*

Pre-screen applicants with assessment for job fit

About $300 for advertising

Evaluation

Is it worth the time, money, & effort required to complete it? Yes [x] No [ ]

Is it the right time for the goal? Yes [x] No [ ]

Action Steps *(What do you have to do to accomplish it?)*	Person Responsible	Amount of Time	Target Date
1. Develop Job Description, competencies needed for the job, and revise compensation plan.	Me	2 hours	Sept. 3
2. Develop the pre-screen and interview script with behavioral-based questions that are aligned with the competencies.	Me	2 hours	Sept. 7
3. Send out email to my contact list asking for referrals	Me	30 min.	Sept. 7
4. Write the ad and advertise on social media and LinkedIn	Assistant	1 hour	Sept. 7
5. Screen candidates and set up qualified candidates for the assessment.	Assistant	3 hours	Sept. 15
6. Go through the assessment results and identify the most qualified based on background, pre-screen interview, and job fit assessment.	Me	2 hours	Sept. 20
7. Set up interviews with the top three to five candidates	Assistant	1 hour	Sept. 24
8. Conduct interviews	Me	8 hours	Sept. 28
9. Check references	Assistant	5 hours	Oct. 6
10. Finalize compensation plan and send offer letter	Me	1 hour	Oct. 8
11. Put together two-day training agenda, plan, and sales and product training material	Me/Assistant	8 hours	Oct. 18
12. Introduce new hire to staff, conduct two days of training and review ninety-day checklist	Me	16 hours	Oct. 25
13. Set up regular training schedule (with topics identified) with new employee by meeting once a week for two hours for the next ninety days.	Me	24 hours	Jan. 25

Sacrifices/Trade-offs *(What will you need to give up in order to accomplish it?)*

Since this project will take 73.5 hours of my time – I will need to ask my business partner to handle the xyz project and deliver ABC's training for the next six weeks.

GOAL/PROJECT PLANNING WORKSHEET

Today's Date:	Target Date:	Actual Completion Date:
Estimated Time to Complete:	Estimated Cost:	Personal: _____ Business: _____

Goal/Project *(What do you want to accomplish?)*

Benefits *(Why do you want it?)*	**Consequences** *(What could you lose?)*
Obstacles *(What's keeping you from reaching this goal?)*	**Solutions** *(How will you overcome the obstacles?)*

Resource List *(What do you need to accomplish it? Money, Time, People, Things?)*

Evaluation

Is it worth the time, money, & effort required to complete it? Yes [   ] No [   ]

Is it the right time for the goal? Yes [   ] No [   ]

Action Steps *(What do you have to do to accomplish it?)*	Person Responsible	Amount of Time	Target Date

Sacrifices/Trade-offs *(What will you need to give up in order to accomplish it?)*

LEADERSHIP EXERCISES
FUTURE DIRECTED

Leadership Exercise #12: WHERE I STAND NOW

Exercise Purpose: To assess where you stand now in relation to where you would like to be. By assessing all areas of your life, you will begin to see trends that add clarity, focus, and foundation to your life plan.

Expected Outcome: To write down thoughts about where you currently stand in all areas of your life so that goals can be identified and planned. On the next page is the full chart for all of the areas in your life where you may want to set goals. Before you set the goals, however, do a self-analysis (Where I Stand Now) chart to help you determine a starting point. Below is a sample of what some of the items on your chart may look like:

WHERE I STAND NOW

Area of Life	What is going right?	What is going wrong?	What is confusing?	What is missing?	What needs changing?
Health	Just started using my treadmill again	Eating too many sweets			Need to eat more healthy and cut out sweets
Friends and Family	Good relationships	I never see my sister	Should I travel to her or have her come to me?	Time spent with sister	Trade off every six months traveling to see sister
Spouse or Significant Other	Great dating relationship				
Financial	Handling all my expenses	Not saving for future	Whether I should get a loan to get my MBA		Stop eating out every night in order to save money

WHERE I STAND NOW

Area of Life	What is going right?	What is going wrong?	What is confusing?	What is missing?	What needs changing?
Health					
Friends and Family					
Spouse or Significant Other					
Financial					
Career or Job					
Personal Growth and Learning					
Environment					
Spiritual					
Fun & Recreation					

Now take a look at what you've written. What stands out as positives? Gaps? Concerns? Conflicts? What goals and actions should come from your thinking? Write down your thoughts below:

_____

_____

_____

_____

_____

_____

_____

_____

_____

_____

You may have more power in your life than you think! Take a look at your current reality (previous page), and the vision you have for your life. What, if anything, can you do about these discrepancies?

On a scale of 0-100, rate your current satisfaction and fulfillment with your life, personally and professionally, by marking an "x" on that spot on the line below. Then, identify where you would *like* it to be and place an "x" on that spot.

0_____100

Now ask, "What is keeping me from reaching the higher point on the scale?" List all the factors you can think of on the left side. On the right side, list all the strengths and resources you have to help you change and/or cope with these factors.

1._____ 1._____

2._____ 2._____

3._____ 3._____

4._____ 4._____

5._____ 5._____

Now go back and put a plus by those factors you feel you have power to change, and a minus by those you feel you have absolutely no power to control at all.

Based upon this exercise, create goal planning sheets for the following top three goals:

1._____

2._____

3._____

Competency Eight
SELF-DISCIPLINE

In this Chapter, we will:

- Identify the benefits to being self-disciplined.

- Learn about the six key ingredients that must be in our lives to allow for self-discipline to flourish.

- Learn tips for managing time more effectively.

- Identify priorities (the highest payoff type of activities that are most likely to help you reach your goals.)

- Help you detect the triggers to negative emotional responses and strategies to stay in emotional control.

- Give you three exercises to help you get and stay disciplined.

Chapter Eight
SELF-DISCIPLINE

Don't finish where you started.

If you were to decide today to build your own home, what's the first thing you would do? You would probably want to start by first picturing in your mind exactly how you want your house to look, along with a few must-have features. You would consider how many bedrooms and bathrooms you want, where you want the laundry room located, and maybe even details like what kind of lighting fixtures you'll use. The next step after visualizing your dream home would be to find out from builders the general price range to build a house of this size, get plans drafted, and start preparing for the design and building of your home. There is a process to building a home so that the final structure is a close resemblance to the home imagined in the beginning, plus a few modifications along the way as challenges unfold.

The same principles apply to building personal leadership and improving self-discipline. You wouldn't begin to build your own home by just picking up a hammer and nailing two boards together. Yet, this is what people often do in planning their careers and life. They just hammer away on nebulous activities, often without a plan in the hopes that they can build something good.

To build a life that will result in the accomplishment of your dreams and the fulfillment of your values, requires you to effectively lead the most important person of all—you. This chapter will show you how to develop *self-discipline*. Self-discipline is the foundation of all of the other character competencies. You will only be able to lead others if you are able to follow the discipline of being a good leader for yourself.

For many people, competition towards others is the name of the game. Even within the same organizations, individuals spend most of their time competing with each other for power, rank or privilege. But being a good leader begins with *self*-competition. The real question is not did I win, but how did I do *today* compared to my goal? It doesn't make sense to compare yourself to others because you can only control your *own* performance. Another person's goal or performance may be less than what the organization needs, so if you beat them, you may still fall short of what the organization requires of you. A commitment to being self-discplined means you will try to do better today than you did yesterday.

Although most formal leadership roles begin and end with the working day, self-discipline is constant. It encompasses every facet of life; it involves every action, thought, or attitude of every waking hour. We have said that personal leadership is not what you do, but who you are – at home, at work, in your social environment and when you are alone. Any plan for development of personal leadership involves the whole person. Let's talk about how to develop your self-discipline.

Your Personal Plan for Leadership Action

First, how would you like your life to look? Imagine that you are being interviewed by a well-respected author/writer at your retirement party years from now. What would you like to be able to tell that writer about your accomplishments in life? About the things you did and the problems you solved? If the writer were interviewing your employees, clients, boss, or coworkers, what would you want them to say about you?

If you're not sure where to start, we recommend participating in a normative professional assessment to determine your personal strengths and weaknesses. Normative means that it is not based solely on your opinion of yourself, as with the assessment in the beginning of this book, but based on the population in the rest of the world, country, or possibly the job that you now occupy. Be sure the assessment you choose has a high-data reliability so you can better trust the results. This will give you the foundation to know where to start with your personal development plan. Knowing where you are in your own character competencies is like the "you are here" symbol on a mall kiosk map. It is the reference point from which progress can now be defined and made.

In addition, reflect on your own list of values as introduced in Chapter Three. They will help you determine what is important to you. Your values also help you identify your priorities so you're not wasting time on activities that won't get you anywhere.

Self-discipline can be one of the most powerful paths to happiness that also garners respect from those around you. When you are self-disciplined, you act in alignment with your values and goals by following through on the right activities or tasks, regardless of whether you like them or not. You are able to overcome weaknesses and pursue what you know is right despite temptations to abandon it.

Self-discipline is the ability to move from emotion to logic and from logic to action. It's doing the things that you know you have to do to reach goals. And self-discipline is made up of good habits.

Consider improving your self-discipline as a type of selective training in creating new habits of thought, speech, and action toward improving yourself. There are many benefits to being self-disciplined.

Self-discipline is what helps us:

1. **Avoid regrets from acting rashly and on impulse.**

2. **Build self-esteem by fulfilling promises that are made to ourselves and others.**

3. **Achieve goals by continuing to work on a project, even after the initial rush of enthusiasm has faded away.**

4. **Capitalize on opportunities by not succumbing to laziness and procrastination.**

5. **Acquire knowledge by reading a book, and remain tuned in and engaged with it all the way to the last page.**

6. **Get noticed by other leaders in the organization as someone who is reliable and trustworthy.**

The list of benefits to being self-disciplined can go on for pages. A leader who desires to pursue her dreams and reach her potential will experience limitless benefits if she practices the self-discipline required to get there. With the base quality of self-discipline strongly intact, we can advance in our personal leadership plan with resolve and gusto.

If you struggle with self-discipline, the good news is that it can be practiced and learned. Beating yourself up over it is unlikely to help, as it will most likely make you feel de-motivated and possibly even depressed (depending on the extent this habit has affected your career or life). Instead, bear in mind that it's not unusual to feel undisciplined. Many people feel they need improvement in their self-discipline and willpower. That's why we offer leadership exercises so you can practice your willpower and form positive habits to maintain it. Self-discipline can be developed for achieving the many goals that you dare to dream.

In the beginning, you will require constant motivation to perform acts of self-discipline until these acts become habitual and don't require any conscious thought. Strategies to motivate yourself can include reading books, visualization, writing down your dreams, watching uplifting podcasts or Ted Talks. It can also include talking with someone who inspires you or helps you think through your goals towards mastering self-discipline.

It is vital to note the six key ingredients that need to be present in our lives for us to excel in self-discipline. Many people already have all six of these key ingredients but may lack the knowledge of where, when, and how to use them. These ingredients include:

- Motivation – the reason for doing anything that fuels our effort and makes goals worth achieving.

- Goals – those tangible achievements that form our definition of success and happiness, and are understood with perfect clarity.

- Time Management – the ability to focus and act on what is important in the midst of the multiple urgencies or opportunities that present themselves daily.

- Self-Control – the act of controlling our emotions, actions, thoughts, words, and personal direction.

- Measurement – Using the right scales or measurement tool to allow for self-discipline or habits to flourish.

- Perseverance – That attachment to a meaningful purpose that drives people to keep moving towards a goal despite obstacles, fears, frustrations, or boredom that might cause them to give up.

When a leader executes all six of these ingredients, then self-discipline is most likely achieved. Since the first two ingredients—motivation and goals—have been discussed in previous chapters, the focus in this chapter will be on the remaining four ingredients: Time Management, Self-Control, Measurement, and Perseverance.

Time Management

Because time is so precious, fleeting, and nonrenewable, the ability to manage time and control actions that consume time is critical. You must also make choices about what is important, and use time where it has the most positive impact.

Understanding your highest priority or pay-off activities as a leader and aligning others to understand theirs is the mark of leadership effectiveness. Think about it. The only way for a company or organization to make a profit is if employees are spending time in activities that are worth *more* than their rate of pay. Identifying activities that will actually make the organization more profitable is the key to prioritizing. Some of these high priority activities for leaders in organizations may include:

- planning and organizing
- communicating
- staff development and training
- holding others accountable for results
- hiring effectively
- motivating people

Leaders who are equipped with resources (assessments, exercises, etc.) will be able to ensure the most qualified person is accomplishing these activities within an organization. As well, leaders themselves must be intentional about spending adequate time defining and contributing to their priorities. To be successful managing time, there are a few rules of thumb to be aware of when setting priorities or high-payoff activities.

Don't try to schedule yourself too tightly or with more work than can be thoroughly completed in a reasonable workday. Recognize the amount of necessary interruptions in the flow of a workday by tracking your interruptions. If the average number of interruptions amounts to two hours a day, then schedule work based upon a six-hour day versus an eight-hour day.

Carefully define your priorities. What makes an activity a priority is that it is directly and definably connected to a goal. Don't fall prey to engaging initially in tasks that are fun, interesting, familiar, or easy, and then calling them priorities.

One of the most common thieves of time is distraction. To manage your time well, expect distractions and develop strategies to deal with them. We have identified some of the most familiar, and time sucking, distractions. We'll begin with the unavoidable crisis.

First of all, let us point out that everything is not a crisis. Let's amend that slightly... not everything that everyone else brings to you as a crisis, is a crisis. Proper crisis identification is essential to time management. Strategizing ahead of time on how to qualify derailments of productivity will save you from dropping what you are working on in order to focus on the crisis.

Be prudent to not overuse or cloud the level of a crisis with inappropriate emotional descriptors that add false urgency such as debilitating, catastrophic, or fiasco. A broken finger on a construction site is not catastrophic. A load of raw materials that arrives four hours late is frustrating, but certainly not debilitating. A donor heart that shows up four hours late may qualify as debilitating.

Another distraction is the challenge of concentration, or the lack of it. Adult ADD or simple fatigue, burnout or sensory overload (television, cell phones, internet, etc.) can derail your ability to concentrate. Strategy: Along with the obvious strategy of getting adequate sleep, also consider de-cluttering. Although subconscious, clutter is a visual chaos trigger that aggravates a mental feeling of being out of control, and managing this feeling takes energy. De-cluttering can look like having an organized desk, home, or car and it can also include sending repeated junk mail to spam. Also consider only checking your email twice in the morning and twice in the afternoon rather than checking every ten

> **The word EVENTUALLY engulfs hope and empowers hope. On the sinister and deceptive side, this simple word gives people the perpetual option to take action someday in the future, and as long as the option remains real, people are robbed of the motivation and need to take action now.**

minutes. Changing activities is like retooling a production line. The transition itself yields nothing and wastes both energy and time.

A subtle, yet defeating, distraction is the mindset of *eventually*—one of the most bipolar words known to man. *Eventually* means the status quo is acceptable for an indefinite period of time. *Eventually* is disrespectful to one's dreams because it reduces the importance of a dream to where it isn't worthy of action today. *Eventually* is not bound by time because it always connects a person's life to a future hope with such great clarity, that the option becomes more important than the reality.

Think of all the things people will eventually do. They will eventually lose weight, get their Master's degree, repair a relationship, get braces to improve their smile, or become self-employed and work for themselves with that one great idea that came into view twenty-five years ago. Leaders are often quoted as saying "eventually this company will get its act together and start treating people with the respect they deserve," and funny how that never seems to happen *now*, because it can always happen *eventually*.

Conversely, the word *eventually*, when backed up by a very clear goal, action, or productive behavior, can keep your purpose and dreams alive with a vibrant energy that can outlast even the biggest of obstacles. *Eventually* the pediatric wing of a hospital will get funded and built; the plans are in the drawing stages and fundraising efforts have begun. *Eventually* cancer will get cured. *Eventually* a company will go public. A sales manager can rightfully say, "If we keep reaching out to the community, *eventually* somebody is going to say yes to buying our product."

If you knew the option of *eventually* was going to disappear at the end of the business day today, and anything on your list to *eventually* partake in would be gone, how would that influence your time management? Would you make the change now, take action now, invest in the dream now, or forever stay the same because the future option is gone? Would you put down the hamburger and immediately get a salad knowing that after today, there is no option to lose fifty pounds? Would you call a coworker and apologize now knowing there is no time in the future to do it? Would you be more transparent with the people on your team knowing the consequences of living the lie would forever be cemented in stone and the peace and freedom that comes from living your values would be gone? You are either working on your hopes and dreams with definable actions or you are not.

If the word *eventually* crosses your mind, convincing you of the false illusion that the future will allow you to take action later on a dream, then there is room for improvement in your self-discipline. One strategy: Write a list of wants and needs that have been on your *eventually* list for some time. Circle the ones where *eventually* is no longer an option for you. Then download the Employers Edge Goal Planning Form at www.theemployersedge.com and fill out the Goal Planning Form as if the option of setting those goals will expire in the next sixty minutes. Self-discipline *now* means there is no more *eventually*.

The final distraction and time waster we will point out is *paralyzing perfectionism*. This is the erroneous belief that a task can't be completed until it can be done absolutely perfectly. Reason this out. Too many obstacles can surface unexpectedly that may prevent the desired perfect completion. Sure, perfection is the worthy standard in a dire medical procedure or military operation, and criminals walk free when the evidence gathering team isn't perfect, but when perfectionism prevents the start or an advancement towards a goal, it becomes an excuse not a virtue. One rarely has a chance to do something that well, and if too much time is taken, the perfect outcome originally intended to complete is no longer needed. Business and life change too quickly and unexpectedly. If 90% perfection generates as much profit and customer satisfaction as 100% perfection, then plan to complete a task at a perfect 90%, and celebrate if you improve upon that. Just get going.

Here are some steps you can take to turn your distractions into productivity:

1. **Take the first step**. Divide your most intricate tasks into smaller bits so that you do not get overwhelmed. Lead yourself and exercise the self-discipline to take the first step!

2. **Learn how to say *no*.** Saying no to something opens up time to say yes to something else. If you don't learn to say no, you will never have complete control over your time.

3. **Set deadlines for accomplishing tasks**. Without deadlines, your work may be stretched out over too much time.

4. **Make appointments with yourself to do important work.**
   By blocking off appropriate time periods on your calendar,
   you can protect your time just as you would an appointment
   with a client or a vendor.

5. **Don't do jobs that are assigned to others**, or should be
   assigned to others, unless you have a solid reason for helping
   out. If your support staff has been assigned definite responsibilities, don't handle them. It may take a while to train them,
   but the timesavings will continue once they are trained.

6. **Ask yourself often, "Is this the best use of my time right
   now?** Is what I am doing related to my goals? Is there something else I could be doing that would have a greater pay-off?
   Then why am I not doing it right now?"

Successful time management leads to successful self-discipline.
That's worth spending time on, isn't it?

Self-Control

Can a leader be disciplined but lack self-control? Most likely, you
have met this person. He manages his day and his time effectively. He
follows through on projects. He exercises, eats right, and is on time
to every meeting. Yet, when life presents challenges to this person, he
loses control of his emotions and stresses out. He demonstrates his
lack of self-control by isolating himself, or the opposite, by yelling at
whomever crosses his path.

Self-control is the ability to control your emotions, behavior, and
desires in the face of external demands. On the surface, it may seem
that self-control is simply a matter of taking a deep breath and keeping yourself in check when emotions come on strong. While it's true
that self-control in these situations is a formidable challenge, there's
far more to self-control than putting a cork in it when you are about
to blow up or breakdown in tears.

Self-control is necessary for effective self-discipline because it
includes being keenly aware of your feelings. You can only choose
how to actively respond to an emotion when you're aware of it. Since
we're hard-wired to experience emotions before we can respond to
them, it's the one-two punch of reading emotions effectively and
then controlling the reaction to them that sets the best leaders apart.

A high level of self-control assures you aren't getting in your own way and acting irrationally. It also assures you aren't frustrating other people to the point that they resent, disrespect, or dislike you. When you understand your own emotions and can respond to them the way you choose, you have the power to take control of difficult situations, react nimbly to change, and take the initiative needed to achieve your goals.

On the other hand, when you don't stop to think about your feelings—including how they are influencing your behavior, and will continue to do so in the future—you set yourself up to be a frequent victim of emotional hijackings. Whether you're aware of it or not, your emotions can control you.

What makes controlling your emotions even more complicated is that at the core level of our humanity we all want to be right and validated. So we reach out to people to validate our anger, depression, and fear so we can justify these bad behaviors in bigger doses. With the support of another's validation, you may see your anger, depression, or fear as perfectly natural and warranted, so there is no will to change.

We love this old Cherokee Native American proverb:

> *An old Cherokee is teaching his grandson about life.*
>
> *"A fight is going on inside me," he tells the boy. "It is a terrible fight, and it is between two wolves. One is evil – he is anger, envy, sorrow, regret, greed, arrogance, self-pity, guilt, resentment, inferiority, lies, false pride, superiority and ego."*
>
> *The old chief continues, "The other is good – he is joy, peace, love, hope, serenity, humility, kindness, benevolence, empathy, generosity, truth, compassion and faith."*
>
> *He looks at his grandson and says, "The same fight is going on inside you – and inside every other person, too."*
>
> *The grandson thinks about this for a moment and then asks his grandfather, "Which wolf will win?"*
>
> *The old Cherokee simply replies, "The one you feed."*

Being able to control your emotions depends in large part on how much you feed a particular emotion, on how much you focus on what you are afraid of, enraged by, or depressed about. If you know

199

the destructive wolf is being fed, even validated, in your own life be honest with yourself. You are on the wrong path and you need to fix that. Good self-control requires that we understand our own emotions or moods, recognizing when and why we are upset and having very real strategies in place to be able to influence the way that we feel.

I (Ed) was coaching a Vice President of Administration in a large corporation. He had a problem of lashing out in anger at his team and his peers. He would lose composure in team meetings, over the phone, one-on-one, and would leave people crying and wanting to quit. What's worse was the effect it was having on his direct reports' work performance. When his people looked at the contributions they'd made to the company and realized this VP would rarely affirm them for it, their attitude grew into a "what's the point anyway" perception of their value. They became very defeatist and minimalistic.

The problem had persisted for some time and the VP's bosses were losing faith in his ability to ever overcome this disruptive problem.

As I began to work with this angry VP, I explained to him that anger, like depression, is often a symptom of a larger problem. I told him there was no sense trying to manage the anger until we discovered the source of it. He was willing to explore why he became angry in certain situations so quickly, and he recognized that he would lose his cool when he was afraid of failing or looking incompetent in front of his peer executives. So we went to work on his fear of failing.

Next, I helped the VP identify and define his values so he could see how his anger is incongruent with his principles. I explained to him, "You have to be so connected to your values that they are top of mind in an anger crisis moment. You want your self-awareness to kick in and say, 'hey, this isn't me.'" It was the value of being a good team leader that really landed with this VP as a reason to overcome anger.

I was able to show him how the people on his team had stopped responding to his leadership, and had actually learned to avoid triggering his anger by sidestepping around him. This observation went completely against the VP's value of being a good leader. As he became aware of his values and how he needed to change his mindset, we finally were able to make progress on subduing his anger.

So rather than feeding the wolf, get ahead of the negative emotions by identifying the triggers that cause the negative emotional response. When someone tells you that they cannot meet a deadline, for example. This will help you become self-aware when the negative emotion hits you in the future. And as you identify positive, actionable responses to each trigger you can form new habits. One such response may be to ask questions to better understand the situation that got you upset. If people are critical towards you, work out how their comments can be constructive and helpful to you. Make time to think about situations and your emotions. Think of ways you could change what you do or the way you react.

In the midst of an intense emotion, examine the feeling and its cause. Then ask yourself, "Is this a healthy feeling?" "How do I want to feel?" "What would make me feel better (that I can control)?" You may come to the conclusion that when you are angry, it is helpful for you to breathe and focus on what is going right in your life. For sure, it is typically a good idea to take time out. Get away from a difficult situation for a short time and get some exercise, drink water, or breathe deeply.

Then change your mood.

We tend to assume that emotions just happen to us and like storms, the best we can do is wait until they pass. But unlike climatic storms, we can influence, even change, our moods without resorting to unhealthy means such as rage, depression, or even extreme resorts such as alcohol or drugs. Don't be passively carried along by the current of the mood. If you are anxious about something, start to imagine that what you are anxious about has already happened and gone much better than expected.

One easy way to alter your mood is to instantly do something else. For example, if you are writing a company newsletter and you're growing frustrated because you can't seem to conjure up content, continuing to sit there will only deepen the emotion. Instead, get up from your computer and go help someone with a project that they are working on. This will inevitably change the way you are feeling.

Finally, ask yourself, "What behavior right here and now will demonstrate to people that my life philosophy really is me?" Remind yourself of your personal values and which value this emotion is violating (such as caring about people, inspiring teamwork, being helpful, etc.)

As you exercise better self-control habits, you will also benefit by understanding how to use the proper scales to determine appropriate actions. Let us explain…

Measurement and The Scales Of Determination

Most leaders really do want to excel in their self-discipline, but at times they fall short because they are making decisions for the wrong reasons. Unbeknownst to many people, there are different scales that are used to measure the payoff for taking an action or not. Some payoff scales motivate people to act consistently with their goals, and other payoff scales actually discourage their goals.

For example, a person is on a diet. And although her goal is to lose weight, she makes the decision to eat based on how hungry she is. Her measurement scale looks like this:

NOT HUNGRY - 1 2 3 4 5 6 7 8 9 10 - VERY HUNGRY.

On a scale of 1-10, if her hunger is raging at a whopping 9, she will choose the drive-thru, even though it's not on her diet plan.

Another dieter may decide that hunger is not a scale that determines if he should eat or not. He's only willing to eat if it tastes good. No need to waste calories on something bland or tasteless. So he decides TASTE is the more relatable scale to determine if he will eat or not. His scale may go from:

NOT TASTY - 1 2 3 4 5 6 7 8 9 10 - VERY TASTY

The bagel from the local bakery may score an 8 in the moment and is therefore very worthy of consumption. In fact anything over a 5 is considered irresistible. So he eats it.

These scales are significant because we all make decisions based on their measurement, whether we know it or not. Too often the wrong scale is used to determine an action in the moment because the correct scale is not determined ahead of time. For example, an athlete is trying to decide if he should work out or not. He worked out the previous day and is evaluating how sore he is today to decide whether he should jump on the exercise bike or head for the locker room. So his scale for today is *NOT SORE – SORE*. He decides that on a scale of 1-10 his thighs are a burning 9, which is too sore to work out so he packs his bag and leaves the gym. But if this athlete were committed to a different predetermined scale, the temporary pain would not sway him. With a simple scale of *NOT A NEED – NEED* firmly in mind, the athlete would assess how much he needed today's workout, regardless of how he felt about it. If he determines his need to exercise at a 6 or higher, he'll be motivated to work out.

Deciding ahead of time what scales and measurements for success that you will use when faced with a "right now" decision will ensure self-discipline. You will make more consistent decisions when you adhere the right scale to achieve a goal, even though it may be difficult.

We see the importance of correct measurement scales in business all of the time. Leaders need to know that they subconsciously set the scales for which they measure themselves, and unless they switch from destructive subconscious scales to identifiable conscious productive scales, they tend to flounder in the leadership role until the misery overtakes them and they move on. It's not that they lacked competency or weren't responsible, but instead they often measured themselves against the wrong scales and this inhibited their effectiveness.

I (Ed) was asked by a professional to coach him in his leadership business development role. It was a new position in the organization, and he was struggling with the new perceptions of him that he thought came with this new role. When asked several questions, he commented that he didn't want to be perceived as a nuisance, a peddler with no perceived product or service value. This mindset influenced his level of confidence in engaging in the sales process, which terribly impacted his team. He was asked on a scale of 1-10, how he rated salespeople as a perceived nuisance (LOW NUISANCE – HIGH NUSIANCE). He answered as an 8. Likewise he scored himself a 9 on the receiving rejection scale (LOW REJECTION – HIGH REJECTION). He then scored himself a 4 on the scale of LOW PERCEIVED VALUE – HIGH PERCEIVED VALUE, and LOW CONFIDENCE – HIGH CONFIDENCE. No wonder he was stymied by the sales process and experiencing the lack of sales success. The scales by which he measured himself offered a convincing argument to not sell, to not take action.

This business development manager was then asked on a scale of 1-10, how much actual real value was there in the service his organization provided the market (NOT VALUABLE – VERY VALUABLE). He scored on this scale a 10. He was then asked on a scale of 1-10, how important was it to himself and the organization that he pick up the phone to hunt for business and make new contacts (NOT IMPORTANT – VERY IMPORTANT). He scored on this scale a 10 again. Lastly, he was asked on a scale of 1-10, what was his ability to solve client problems (LOW ABILITY – HIGH ABILITY). He scored on this scale a 10, and said that it was their competitive strength.

He started to see the importance of judging himself with the proper scale. Since he was so good at providing value and solving problems, these scales became the new driving relevance to developing business. The "nuisance" scale and the "perceived value" scale didn't even apply anymore, so when the moment of truth came, and it was time to pick up the phone to contact a potential client or assist a team member in doing the same task, the previous destructive self-talk no longer applied. He decided he would evaluate himself on the more applicable scales (reasons) for calling people. His company needs him to call people he doesn't know, he provides a grand value, and he solves problems, therefore he makes the calls and engages in sales conversations, all by predetermining the proper measurement scales.

The scales that leaders identify with will determine their success by determining their level of belief and actions.

Perseverance

What is the difference between determination and perseverance? Determination has a decision element tied to it. When you determine to take action, you're making a decision to do so. Perseverance is continuing in that course of action without regard to discouragement, opposition or previous failure.

Imagine this. You want to become an entrepreneur. Maybe you always have, or maybe this is a new discovery for you. Either way, you find yourself in a bad position to do anything entrepreneurial. Let's say that you are saddled with debt. You live an hour away from any major city. You have ten kids with one on the way. And you've also recently been in an accident that resulted in a severed limb.

Talk about hardship. That sounds like a tough situation for sure;

however, if you really want it and are willing to persevere, you will get it. You will find a way or you will make a way. You will continue on despite any obstacle or discouragement until you make it to your goal. Whether your goal is to lose weight, complete projects on time, be a better leader, spouse or parent, or spend less time playing computer games or on social media, the critical step is to resist short-term temptations in order to meet long-term goals.

I (Ed) used to coach youth wrestling. One of my wrestlers would be on the mat, face down with his opponent on top of him. The opponent would press his forearm against the back of my wrestler's head, holding him immobilized. I could see my brave little athlete looking up at me in the corner, mouthing the words "what do I do?"

This was a common situation for all of the boys. Whenever they would get caught in tough holds, they would look towards me for advice. What they wanted was a direction to free themselves of their precarious circumstances, but the only right answer I was able to give them in that moment was: KEEP MOVING.

In wrestling, allowing yourself to stay hopelessly immobilized gives your opponent unlimited license to overpower you however he sees fit, and that never ends well. Staying hopelessly immobilized as a leader gives the universe unlimited license to abuse you however it sees fit as well, and that never ends well either. Have you ever noticed yourself stifled, looking for a direction to move, but feeling paralyzed to do anything at all? For example, you've been assigned to improve an antiquated process or product, but you don't know what to do. Or your company is shutting down operations at your division, and you know that you need to look for a new job, but you don't know where to start. Have you found yourself saying any of the following things?

- "I can't get this report done until my boss gives me the financials."

- "I can't make my first sales appointment until I fully understand and know how to pitch our products."

- "I don't even know where to start."

- "I can't ask anyone out on a date until I lose weight."

- "If I only had a down payment, I could afford to buy a house."

- "If we had a decent website, we could probably get more business."
- "I can't take on that project until I can get some of my day-to-day responsibilities off of my plate."

Does this sound a little like the blame game from Chapter Five? Imbedded in the blame game is the message "I'm paralyzed and can't move." As simple as it sounds, the first step to your solution is to keep moving. And if you've stopped, get moving again. Perseverance requires a mindset of *do something. Anything.*

In wrestling, I would tell my boys, "Your opponent will only reveal a weakness or an opportunity when you take an action first." I explained that the opponent's weakness would become their next direction to exploit. "Step one to getting out of a bind is to get your legs back underneath you (base up) so you can provide yourself with options in your next move."

I would tell my wrestlers to shoot high, shoot low, move left, move back. And in doing so, their opponent will reveal they are slower to respond to one of these advances. Human nature drives us to set the direction first so we know what action to take second. However, sometimes the action reveals the direction. Take an action first, any action, and then look for the weakness or opportunity the universe shows you.

Doing something, anything, may look like meeting somebody new, calling a friend to practice your new product pitch, reading a book, or calling a lender to get pre-qualified to buy a house. This is the equivalent to moving left, moving right, moving backwards and seeing how your opponent (the universe, the culture) responds. When you are stifled in business or in life and you don't know what to do or where to go, just remember to always *keep moving*, and the direction towards your goals will undoubtedly show up.

One of the world's great philosophers Anon said, "Of all the people you will know in a lifetime, you are the only one on this earth that you will never leave nor lose. To the question of your personal leadership, you are the only answer. To the problems of your life you are the only solution."

When you first grasp the full meaning of those statements, you begin to see yourself with a sense of awe and self-reliance. You begin to look inward for guidance and leadership. You understand the absolute necessity for defining your own values, setting progressively higher goals, and structuring a plan for their attainment. You search for purpose and meaning in life. And you find within yourself a wellspring of motivation urging you to contribute to life something uniquely yours.

Like building a home, there is a process to building or developing your future, so the end product closely resembles the ideas in the beginning, and the plan can be lived in every day. When your personal life is in balance, because *you* have chosen to control its direction and accept responsibility, virtually anything is possible.

ADVICE FROM YOUR COACH

Self-Discipline can be learned, but it takes a reason, a goal, time-management, self-control, and perseverance. Don't expect overnight changes and be patient with yourself as you cultivate new habits. You are worth it!

LEADERSHIP EXERCISES
SELF-DISCIPLINE

Leadership Exercise #13: HIGH PAYOFF ACTIVITIES EXERCISE

Exercise Purpose: To increase individual productivity by engaging in the most profitable activities. To develop the mindset of always questioning if you are acting most productively.

Expected Outcome: High payoff activities are those activities that produce the greatest profits for the organization. Simply measured, the only way for a company to make a profit is if every employee is spending time in activities that are worth more than their rate of pay. The purpose of this exercise (on the next 2 pages) is to define both the most important high payoff activities, and the less profitable, less important, low or lower payoff activities that may need to be delegated or simplified. Once completed, it will prove quite valuable to gain clarity and alignment with team members to share your high and low payoff activities, with the goal of defining theirs as well.

Examples of high payoff activites may include but are not limited to:

- Training and developing my direct reporting staff.
- Planning with my team – including annual, quarterly, and monthly follow-up to goals.
- Problem solving around customer and employee issues.
- Developing new business for the company and securing commitments.
- Completing month end reports by the 5th of the following month.
- Developing specific strategies and plans to improve customer satisfaction.
- Identifying industry trends that may impact the business.
- Developing a new product to replace the old outdated process.

HIGH PAYOFF ACTIVITES

Based on my rate of pay, my time is worth $_____ per hour. Therefore, every activity I perform in my job that is worth *more* than my hourly rate is bringing value (profit) to the company.

If I had to pick only five activities (in order of importance) that are worth more than my rate in pay, they would be:

_____
_____
_____
_____
_____

Is my manager in agreement with these top five? How do I know? Should I ask?

Things I will do to spend more time in my high payoff activities include:

_____
_____
_____
_____
_____
_____

LOW PAYOFF ACTIVITIES

Based on my rate of pay, my time is worth $_____ per hour. Therefore, every activity I perform in my job that is worth *less* than my hourly rate is costing my company profit.

If I had to pick five activities that I am currently performing in my job that are worth less than my rate in pay, they would be:

_____
_____
_____
_____
_____

Is my manager in agreement with these bottom five? How do I know? Should I ask?

Things I will do to spend less time in my low pay-off activities include:

_____

_____

_____

_____

_____

_____

_____

Leadership Exercise #14: STRESSORS EXERCISE

Exercise Purpose: To learn how to most effectively manage stress.

Exercise Outcome: Attain clarity with both the specific causes of stress and the solution to overcome or manage that stress. Break stress down into its individual components and then develop a simple plan to eliminate the stress.

In the following chart, write down all the things in specific areas of your life that are causing you a significant amount of stress. Next to the stressor, write down the things that you can do to take charge of that situation. Each time you are stressed, choose to grab ahold of it by writing down your thoughts. Clearly defined thoughts will motivate you to take action and get back in charge of your life.

STRESSORS CHART

	STRESSORS	WHAT I CHOOSE TO DO...
FAMILY		
FINANCIAL		
JOB/CAREER		
SOCIAL		
SPIRITUAL		
HEALTH		
PERSONAL DEVELOPMENT		
ENVIRONMENT		

Leadership Exercise #15: EMOTIONAL RESPONSE TRACKER

Exercise Purpose: To take control of your emotional responses.

Expected Outcome: To identify the results of emotional responses to people or things that may trigger a negative response. By tracking your results, you train yourself to respond in a more productive way that demonstrates self-control.

Directions:

1. Fill out the first box called My Values by identifying the most important behaviors you expect from yourself as well as in other people that you most effectively work with. (See more on values in Chapter Three.)

2. Think back over the last month or so about the times when people have "pushed your buttons."

3. Identify the situation or event that triggered an emotional response.

4. Identify the feeling you were experiencing.

5. Write down how you handled it (positively or negatively).

6. Identify whether you are happy or not happy with your response by writing in a yes or no.

7. Ask yourself if your response was consistent with the behavioral expectations you have of others, or whether you violated your own values as listed in the chart.

8. Decide how you would like to respond next time if the situation were to come up again.

9. Determine any actions that you would like to take as a result of thinking this through.

Example: EMOTIONAL RESPONSE TRACKER

My Values *(What behaviors are important?):*
Honesty, team player, transparency, caring, productive, timely, competent, trustworthy

	SITUATION #1	SITUATION #2	SITUATION #3
1. The Situation or Trigger	*My business partner said that we need to lease out office space rather than save the space for growth.*		
2. What I Was Feeling	*Concerned that if we lease out the space we won't have enough room to hire additional employees.*		
3. How I Handled It (Results, Emotions, Words, Actions)	*I told him in a demanding sort of way that "we must charge at least $19.50 per square foot to break even, and that we can't lease out more than 1400 square feet."*		
4. Am I Happy w/ Response?	*No*		
5. What I Wish I Would Have Done Differently	*I wish that I had asked him: "Why do you think we need to lease out the extra office space?" And listen to his thinking rather than interject my opinion before hearing his.*		
6. Did I Violate My Values?	*Yes, I was not "caring," and the conversation would have been more "productive" had I listened first.*		
7. What Action Will I Take	*I will go apologize and then ask him for his thoughts on leasing out space.*		

EMOTIONAL RESPONSE TRACKER

My Values *(What behaviors are important?):*			
	SITUATION #1	SITUATION #2	SITUATION #3
1. The Situation or Trigger			
2. What I Was Feeling			
3. How I Handled It (Results, Emotions, Words, Actions)			
4. Am I Happy w/ Response?			
5. What I Wish I Would Have Done Differently			
6. Did I Violate My Values?			
7. What Action Will I Take			

Chapter Nine
LEADERS DEVELOPING
LEADERS

A coach causes others to think, then moves them to action.

Coach or be coached? Both are great ways to get and stay in leadership shape. Through our years of coaching experiences, we can safely say that the *best* way to get into leadership shape and stay there is to coach others. So we would answer this question with the directive: "Be coached *and* coach!"

I, Janet, started coaching leaders, managers, and executives twenty-five years ago. I had difficulty coaching others in areas where I was weak, such as time management, listening skills, confidence, delegation, and organization. It was tempting to be in a coaching session and want to relate to my coachee by saying, "Me too, I am horrible at that!" But that would have been making the coaching about me instead of them. I had to continually remind myself that coaching someone wasn't about whether I was perfect at the skill, but what mattered was whether I was a good coach and whether I had the skills and exercises to give someone else an experience that would hone and develop their skills.

As the years have unfolded, and I look back on having personally coached over 2,000 leaders, executives, CEOs, and sales professionals, I realize and can feel really good about being able to say along with the people that I have coached, "I have become a better leader and human being for it."

In the process of coaching others, the leader as coach sharpens her own beliefs and attitudes about how to self-manage as well as lead others. And as she grows personally her effectiveness as coach improves. In short, coaching helps both the coach and the coachee. And let's face it, there is a crucial need for qualified coaches all around us.

Leaders, managers, and coaches, if not careful, can experience the deception of thinking they are doing a better job than they actually are. Not to blame coworkers for the illusion. Many company cultures set themselves up for this deception to happen.

The population as a whole in many organizations has a political motive from which to give praise and feedback, so the structure itself isn't set up for truthful verbal communication as to how talents are perceived. Feedback is tainted or not fully uncovered because most people just won't give it. Some cultures treat feedback as direct insubordination. So leaders are fooled into believing what a good leader and manager they are, and the deception prevents that person from pursuing a path of development. After all, why train to get good at something that you already believe you are good at?

Often, leaders and managers take on the role of leadership with the assumption they already know how to lead. Their leadership ability is determined by their own perception of their ability. They stand in front of the mirror role-playing their position in a goal-setting meeting and they adopt the "I am leader" persona. Their opinion of their leadership is predicated on the notoriety of being the person in charge, leading a group of knowledge hungry managers into the golden pond of realization. In reality, the oblivious leaders are leading followers into the unknown. To compound the problem, associates sometimes placate these leaders, falsely complimenting their leadership, or they remain silent, perpetuating the leaders' inaccurate view of their leadership ability.

If not careful, the American Idol Effect takes root (see Chapter Six on Influence), and the years of incorrect conditioning to believe they are good leaders can be a substitute for actual leadership and management ability. As this carries on over time, the leaders or managers think they are doing a fantastic job because, after all, nobody said otherwise.

So how do you know the *true* condition of your leadership? When life seems relatively smooth and progress in business is being made, how can a leader recognize his deficiencies? How does a leader know to even look when it doesn't occur to him to look? We would say a wise leader is someone who will seek a trustworthy person to help him recognize his strengths, point out his weaknesses and hold him accountable for managing them. The ripple effect this bold step can create is astounding, and it is altering businesses in a powerful way. As one leader within the organization begins to improve his or her character competencies, the weaknesses of others become more noticeable. And awareness is the first step to positive change, for an individual as well as a business.

Successful organizations incorporate a *leaders coaching leaders* culture. The same principles apply to families and communities. As coach, an experienced leader helps support another leader with truthfulness and guidance. Interestingly, this responsibility increases the effectiveness of the coach as well. It becomes difficult for the coach to hold someone accountable for a competency such as delegation, self-discipline, or managing conflict, if in fact the coach himself isn't demonstrating leadership in that area. An intentional, well-structured coaching mechanism can inspire feedback so course corrections in leadership are revealed sooner rather than later. True, the news may not always be what the coachee wants, but ultimately it will yield benefits for the coachee as well as the organization. Leaders as coaches understand and communicate the goal for which the task is being asked so their team can remain priority focused.

In years past, future executives were groomed within the mid-level management arena of their companies. However, through the flattening of organizations and the re-engineering of corporate structures over the last decade, many companies have reworked how they develop their leaders. Instead of supporting all potential or existing leaders with only group leadership or management training, many companies have chosen to only coach specific executives and leaders to develop a skill or solve a problem because the consequences of sub-standard leadership can no longer be ignored.

Even with limited training budgets, there is still a strong need to provide effective support and mentoring to the leaders of an organization. Consider that four out of ten newly promoted managers and executives fail within eighteen months of starting new jobs, according to research by Manchester, Inc., a leadership development firm in Bala Cynwyd, PA. Failing includes being terminated for performance, performing significantly below expectations or voluntarily resigning from the new position. When newly recruited, the following types of executives experienced the highest failure rates within the first eighteen months: senior-level executives (39%), sales executives (30%), marketing executives (25%), and operations executives (23%).

Increasing numbers of organizations have discovered coaching and mentoring as a highly effective means of helping key players develop leadership skills, achieve business goals, prepare for future challenges, and improve employee retention and engagement. A survey by Manchester Inc. of 100 executives found that coaching provided an average return on investment of almost six times the cost of the coaching. Executives who received coaching benefited by improved:

- Working relationships with direct reports (reported by 77% of executives)

- Working relationships with immediate supervisors (71%)

- Teamwork (67%)

- Working relationships with peers (63%)

- Job satisfaction (61%)

- Conflict reduction (52%)

- Organizational commitment (44%)

- Working relationships with clients (37%)

What becomes evident when considering the outcome this coaching has had on leaders is that all have transformed their managerial style and now use their coaching skills in assisting others with their personal development at work. They reported gains in business performance, quality, organizational strength, customer service, cost-reductions and bottom-line profitability.

If you, or your organization, need help in establishing a *leaders coaching leaders* environment, we strongly urge you to pursue coach training that will provide tools, exercises and skill development. Over our twenty-five years of training leaders in corporations, our clients have witnessed significant improvement in leadership development and measurable growth in revenues and profit. For a fifteen-step plan for how to create a leaders developing leaders culture, visit our website at www.TheEmployersEdge.com.

Now that you have the awareness, the understanding, and some exercises to lead as a coach, it is time to use them to get, and stay, in leadership shape. As you give your leadership a workout, retrain your leadership muscles, and improve your leadership cardio, you will notice others developing a reason to follow your lead. Because it starts with a reason; it always does.

NOTES AND REFERENCES

P.70   Quote from Bill Snyder. K-State Sports Extra, Dec. 21,
       2012, Mark Jannssen

P. 214 **Mark McCormack** (What They Don't Teach You in the
       Harvard Business School) & **Brian Tracy** (Goals!). Other
       self-development gurus that have helped to perpetuate the
       myth include **Zig Ziglar, Tony Robbins** and **Tom Bay**
       in "Look within or Do without."

P. 247 Research conducted by Manchester, Inc., a leadership
       development firm in Bala Cynwyd, PA

P. 248 A survey by Manchester, Inc. of 100 executives coached.

ABOUT THE AUTHORS

Janet McCracken

Janet@TheEmployersEdge.com

Winner of Colorado's Outstanding Woman In Business by the Denver Business Journal, Janet is the CEO of The Employers Edge, a nationally recognized organizational development and talent management company that specializes in leadership and management training, team development, employee assessments, and executive and management coaching. Employers Edge is based in Parker, Colorado, and has additional employees and strategic partners in California, Idaho, Tennessee, South Carolina, and Missouri.

What makes Janet a highly effective and sought-after coach, trainer, and speaker is that, at heart, she is a motivator with a contagious passion and enthusiasm for helping people accomplish their goals. Her mission in life is to be a positive pivotal person in others' lives.

Coming from the corporate world where Janet had held positions including Vice President of Sales and Marketing for a major national company, she launched Employers Edge in 1991. For the last 25 years, Janet's organization has developed people in over 400 corporations including Charter Communication, Lawry's, Starz Entertainment, Toyota, BDO Seidman, Ducommun Technologies, Epson America, U.S. Foodservice, AAA, Celestron, and GE Capital. Janet has personally coached over 2000 CEO's, managers, and sales staff, and facilitates CEO Roundtables, HR Executive Roundtables, and Train the Internal Coach®. She is the author of many award winning training programs which include, The Sales Edge, The Leadership Edge, Teamwork Builders and Blockers, Strategy Management for Teams and more.

Ed Beard

Ed@TheEmployersEdge.com

Ed has a Bachelor of Science degree from Cal Poly State University, San Luis Obispo, CA, where he also returned to coach NCAA Gymnastics while earning his MBA. With a strong sales background beginning in sales management, Ed advanced through the ranks and eventually designed and led business development teams serving large national retailers such as Petco and PetsMart. Conducting over 80 seminars and speaking engagements a year, Ed has the attention of the market on the subjects of training and coaching. Joining Employers Edge as President and co-owner in 2008, Ed has developed multiple training and coaching certification programs, internal coaching structures, and coaching curriculum all focused on empowering people within organizations to endorse strategic performance. Currently leading a CEO Advisory Board in Denver, CO, Ed mentors business owners who need to improve performance in sales, management, operations, and team dynamics.

What makes Ed a highly effective and sought-after coach, trainer, and speaker is that, at heart, he is a teacher and innovator who engages others in possibility thinking and challenges others to have courage and take action.

REQUEST A COACH:

For help getting into leadership shape or to help you through the exercises in this book, go to www.TheEmployersEdge.com and request a coach.

REQUEST THE AUTHORS TO KEYNOTE YOUR NEXT EVENT OR CONFERENCE:

Janet McCracken and Ed Beard have been speaking to groups along with training and coaching leaders for over 25 years. They have helped thousands of leaders discover solutions to business, leadership, and personal challenges.

Janet and Ed bring a highly engaging and interactive keynote that will give your audience a leadership workout, retrain their leadership muscles, and improve their cardio. Janet and Ed explore the eight core character competencies that organizations are quickly adapting as the critical foundation "must haves" in their leaders to advance the culture, drive performance, and support employee retention. Through their stories and leadership exercises, attendees will gain practical tools that they can use to get and stay in leadership shape.

BRING AN EMPLOYERS EDGE TRAINER TO YOUR ORGANIZATION:

With over 40 different ½ day, full day, and 2 day programs, an Employers Edge trainer can create behavior change in your organization in the subjects of management, leadership, sales, teamwork, culture change, performance management, organizational development and strategic planning.

BECOME A LICENSED COACH AND/OR EMPLOYERS EDGE PARTNER:

For more information, other resources, and for dates of public training events and workshops by Ed Beard and Janet McCracken, visit:

www.TheEmployersEdge.com
For more information call (303) 708-8160

CPSIA information can be obtained
at www.ICGtesting.com
Printed in the USA
LVOW04*0010110816
499882LV00006B/9/P